LIFT
OFF

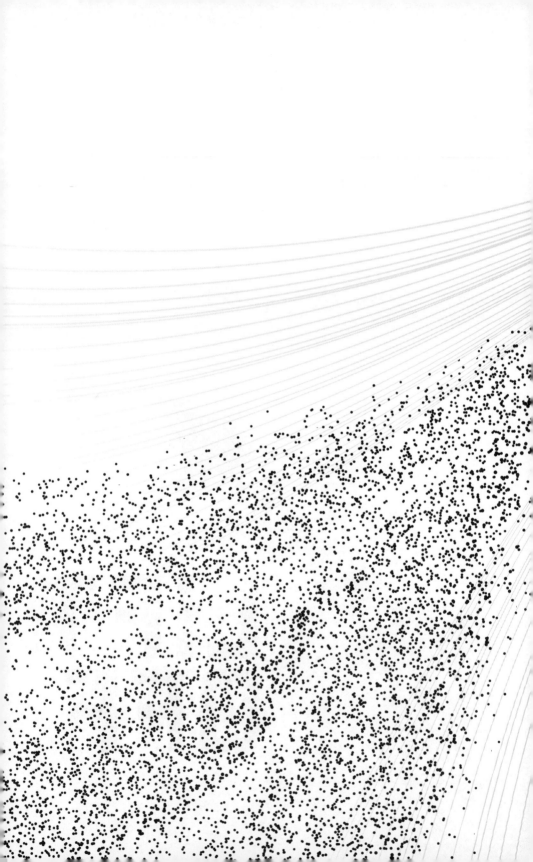

SHARON B. HEATON

LIFT
OFF

12 THINGS TO KNOW BEFORE **SELLING** YOUR BUSINESS

Forbes | Books

Published by Forbes Books, Charleston, South Carolina.
An imprint of Advantage Media Group.

Forbes Books is a registered trademark, and the Forbes Books colophon is a trademark of Forbes Media, LLC.

Printed in the United States of America.

10 9 8 7 6 5 4 3 2 1

ISBN: 979-8-88750-044-7 (Paperback)
ISBN: 979-8-88750-045-4 (eBook)

Library of Congress Control Number: 2023908163

Cover design by Matthew Morse.
Layout design by Matthew Morse.

Since 1917, Forbes has remained steadfast in its mission to serve as the defining voice of entrepreneurial capitalism. Forbes Books, launched in 2016 through a partnership with Advantage Media, furthers that aim by helping business and thought leaders bring their stories, passion, and knowledge to the forefront in custom books. Opinions expressed by Forbes Books authors are their own. To be considered for publication, please visit **books.Forbes.com**.

This book is dedicated to the founders of US-based companies. These are the people who woke up one morning with an idea and did something about it. They sat down at their kitchen table, made plans, took out loans, took risks, and figured stuff out when others said it couldn't be done. They earned some money, paid taxes, and then hired other people who then paid their taxes.

Over years these company founders have taken an idea and, with lots of hard work, worry, and untold frustration, have turned that idea into a company that produces profits. You are the backbone of the American economy, the living embodiment of the American dream!

I also dedicate this book to my mother, Ida Epstein, who showed me how to create a profitable business by deeply caring about her clients and making a difference in their lives.

CONTENTS

PREFACE

If you have picked up this book, let me start by commending you for getting up every day and working on your business. Starting a business is hard. Most people don't do it. Most people who start a company fail. The few who do succeed operate their business for under five years. You have started a business and made it profitable over many years.

Whether you are preparing to sell your business or just thinking about the process of transferring ownership, you are the reason that I wrote this book. I'm passionate about making sure you are treated fairly during every step of the sales process.

I worked for many years in the world of publicly traded companies helping to either buy companies or sell huge entities to the highest bidder. The companies I worked with were often worth billions of dollars. As a corporate lawyer educated at the University of Chicago Law School, I felt a fiduciary responsibility to my clients, but my clients weren't the senior corporate executives I knew. Instead, my clients were massive publicly traded companies and millions of faceless shareholders.

I spent countless hours in rooms filled with lawyers, accountants, and investment bankers doing mergers and acquisition work or "M&A." The piles of paper in conference rooms were high and the days and nights long. Those of us laboring in those rooms were highly educated professionals trying to get a good deal done, but nobody physically present owned majority control of a company.

We talked about what was "best for the shareholders," and people would use words such as "the shareholders believe." Sometimes they would scream "the shareholders have to have" this or that. But the "shareholders" were faceless, and it was easy to think that we worked for the management of the company, not the shareholders. I made a lot of money but found the work unrewarding.

As my career advanced, I began working with privately held companies. Over time my clients became founders or families that had companies with revenues between $10 million and $150 million. Finally, I had found my calling. In 2016 I founded a company called "sbLiftOff" and set up shop in Northern Virginia.

At sbLiftOff, we work with business owners of B2B companies who either want to sell or buy a company. I love my work and think it's important. In fact, helping owners sell their companies and lift off to their next goal in life has become my mission.

Today I am unabashedly dedicated to the founders and owners of middle-market businesses. This book is written for you so you can get the liftoff you deserve.

Here's to your liftoff!
Sharon

INTRODUCTION

You probably have a file in your desk drawer or on your computer where you put materials about selling your company. That file holds information about potential buyers, news on sales in your industry, potential service providers, and random mergers and acquisition (M&A) facts. Now you've picked up this book. So you're obviously curious to learn more and add to that if-I-ever-want-to-sell-and-lift-off-to-something-else file in your head.

You may be the type of person who has already put a lot of time and effort into preparing to sell. You may have already consulted your business partners (if you have them), your lawyer, your accountant, your banker or wealth advisor, your wife or husband, or your trusted college roommate. Whether you feel ready at this point or still have concerns, read on.

There's another way people end up turning to this book. You've had this, "Should I sell?" question rattling around in the back of your brain for some time, but the business has gotten your primary attention.

Then out of the blue, someone has approached you with an offer to buy your company. It's nice that someone has shown interest, but it's also caught you off guard. You don't know where to turn or who you can trust. Maybe you have received a written offer, sometimes in the form of a "letter of intent" (LOI). Even if the offer is acceptable, you worry.

Is it a fair price? Should you go ahead? How should you proceed?

If that's your situation, this is the right book for you. Information is power. Read on.

Regardless of how big your company is, where you are located, or what industry you're in, your company is essentially a machine that takes in revenue and, when working properly, throws off profits.

Maybe your company is a well-oiled machine. Maybe it's a little creaky. But keep this analogy in mind: Your business is a machine. It's terrific to have a business that works like a machine, that takes in revenue and produces profits while you own it. But there is a second layer of value that we're going to explore: Is the machine you've built valuable to someone else?

If your machine itself has value, you can sell it. We're going to discuss how to tell if your business—your cash-generating machine— is valuable and how much it might be worth.

Naturally, you want to get the best deal possible and really understand the terms of that deal. No matter how much planning you've already done or haven't done, there are probably aspects of preparing your company for sale, and going through the M&A journey, of which you're not aware.

That's to be expected. You're likely not a Harvard MBA with decades of M&A experience. This will be your one big M&A transaction, and you need to get it right. This book will guide you, explaining in simple terms *what* you need to do and *how* you need to do it.

You will

- get a general working knowledge of the entire sale process, front to back;
- figure out if the business you now own—that machine that takes in revenue and spins off profit—will have value to a new owner;
- understand how outsiders would calculate the value of your company;
- recognize the potential pitfalls and trade-offs ahead;
- ensure appropriate confidentiality so that word doesn't get out to the wrong people; and
- better handle the normal emotions that every owner feels upon selling their company or business machine.

Are you ready?

It's time to sell your business and lift off to your next stage in life!

CHAPTER 1

FACING YOUR BUSINESS TRANSITION: WHAT IS AHEAD?

Recently, I was on a panel before an audience of business owners. We've all been to these kinds of breakfast events. There is the registration table, the name tags, some scrambled eggs, mini bagels, and weak coffee out of industrial-sized canisters. Up front are the speakers. I participate in these events because I love talking to owners about how to prepare their companies for sale and how to think about the M&A process.

The panel consisted of three professionals: a well-respected commercial banker, a lawyer, and me. When the commercial banker gave his opening remarks, he looked out at the sea of faces and declared,

"M&A isn't an emotional transaction. It's a financial transaction. It's all about the numbers."

I almost laughed out loud. It was as though he was blind to half of what was going on.

My years of experience have taught me that emotions play a vital role in business and even more so when a person like you decides to sell their company. Anyone who has started a company and had success has emotions about that company. If you didn't, you wouldn't be human.

As you move along in this book, I'll introduce you to technical issues that M&A professionals like the people on that morning panel spend a great deal of time on. These include Earnings Before Interest, Taxes, Depreciation, and Amortizations (EBITDAs); multiples and structures; quality of earning; working capital; and all the rest. However, there is an underlying premise that I want you to keep in mind as you think about these numbers and concepts and as you move from chapter to chapter: *like it or not, this will be an emotional transaction for you.*

It's important for you to understand what emotions owners typically experience and how to listen to those feelings but not be guided by your heart solely. In other words, how to make rational decisions that will pay off for you and your family while still feeling good about those decisions.

M&A is often considered the last art of finance. While the focus is often on the word "finance," it is just as important to put the emphasis on the "art."

Why?

Because M&A is not just about numbers. It is also about the art of a successful handoff. M&A involves real-life human beings who are the stakeholders. Powerful emotions such as trust, honesty, fear, and hope are inextricably linked to the sales process. Do not underestimate the importance of people's feelings during an M&A transaction.

So let's take a hard look at your feelings, and let's be honest about them.

Your business has been the focus of your life for years, even decades. Your company is an extension of who you are, and the emotional connection runs bone deep. You have grown your business from concept to a successful reality. There were times you were tempted to give up. People said you couldn't do this and you couldn't do that. You took risks and had highs and lows.

The evolution of your company was almost like raising a child. At the beginning your company was in its infancy. You had minimal revenues and perhaps no employees.

Over time your business grew up. More revenues, more employees, more customers—more headaches! Today your business is transformed from the entity you started. If you had been able to see and understand then what you see now, life would have been easier. But it was a learning curve, a process of discovery, and lots of hard work. Now with a company that in many ways has grown up, you are enjoying the benefits. With a more mature company comes profits and an objective proof of success.

But it's not just about numbers, is it? Some powerful feelings are involved when you think about what it took to get where you are today. Is it any wonder that the idea of transferring your business to another owner feels odd, risky, perhaps even impossible?

It is not unlike the feelings parents have watching their child leave home for the first time. There's the eighteen-year-old high school graduate in the car all loaded up. You know they are old enough. You know they have what they need. You know they must move on. And yet you struggle with a flood of emotions—everything from elation to grief, from swelling pride to dark despair.

These emotions are normal. But no one in their right mind runs out on the driveway and says, "Stop! You can't do this! Don't go to college!"

However, business owners often feel a sudden urge to hold on to their business and end up breaking their deals, unable to go through with it. When that happens, it's expensive, time-consuming, and bad for business.

A client came to my firm a few years after he had gone through a "broken transaction." He explained he had pulled the plug two days prior to close because he panicked at the idea of not having his company.

My client had spent a lot of money on lawyers and accountants. The buyer had spent even more. All that time and expense wasted. All that heartache.

"Can you help me?" he asked. "I want to be able to get through this and feel good about it."

This is not an uncommon situation. Many deals in the lower midmarket do not close. One of the reasons is the inability among the stakeholders to manage their emotions. I knew when I started to work with this seller that he would need help understanding and managing his emotions.

The good news is, there is life after you sell your company.

In fact, some business owners who have sold their companies report a surprising sense of relief and unexpected joy. They will say, "I feel like I'm back in my twenties, with a job but few responsibilities and lots of freedom."

Selling your business has a lot in common with raising kids and sending them off to college or into the work world. The powerful emotions that are stimulated are unavoidable and normal. These emotions need to be recognized, respected, and managed. And just like parents who send their kids out into the world, the next phase of life might surprise them.

Suddenly, time for date night. Suddenly, time for travel. Suddenly, time to work on that project that you've wanted to do but didn't have time, money, or energy to explore. This is ultimately the reason you sell—to lift off to your next adventure in life.

To do that, you will have to manage your emotions.

Scientific studies show that the left side of the brain drives tasks such as logic, analysis, calculation, and risk assessment. By contrast, the right side of the brain powers creativity, emotion, and spontaneity.[1] So you can expect a frequent clash between your logical and emotional brain as the deal goes ahead. Both sides vie to be the primary driver of decision-making. You should expect that and be ready for it.

This is ultimately the reason you sell—to lift off to your next adventure in life.

THE THREE HORSEMEN OF THE APOCALYPSE

As you move back and forth between your logical and emotional sides of your brain, there are three things that attack both sides. I call these the "Three Horsemen of the Apocalypse" in M&As. They are as follows:

- Fear and uncertainty
- Loss of identity
- Feeling judged and inadequate

---

1   Eagle Gamma, "Left Brain vs. Right Brain," May 18, 2021, https://www.simplypsy-chology.org/left-brain-vs-right-brain.html.

FEAR AND UNCERTAINTY

A recent article in *Harvard Business Review* described how Ben Feringa took on fear and uncertainty and ended up winning a Nobel Prize for chemistry. Feringa said he considered himself average. He explained that the secret to his success was not blocking out his fears and uncertainty about his limitations but rather finding ways to calm his fears. He also noted that he relied on "emotional hygiene (attending to emotions—much as you would a physical wound—so that they don't turn into paralyzing self-doubt or unproductive rumination)" and reality checks (putting the ups and downs in perspective).[2]

Just as this chemist did, you, as the owner of a business, have faced fear and uncertainty in the past. Now as you look ahead to your next big experiment, the sale of your business, feeling fear and uncertainty is normal.

Here are some of the fears that many business owners who have successfully sold their companies say they felt:

- "I was afraid of not ever being able to sell."
- "I was afraid I'd sell too low."
- "I was afraid of employees or customers finding out prior to the deal closing."
- "I was afraid of being taken advantage of."
- "I was afraid the buyer didn't really have the cash."
- "I was afraid of some last-minute snag that would keep the deal from going through."

No doubt that you can identify with some, or all, of these. You probably have other fears you can add to the list.

---

2   Nathan Furr and Susannah Harmon Furr, "How to Overcome Your Fear of the Unknown," July–August 2022, https://hbr.org/2022/07/how-to-overcome-your-fear-of-the-unknown.

FDR famously said, "We have nothing to fear except fear itself."[3] It was a rhetorical line, not completely true. Of course, business owners must rationally assess their fear. But it's also true that fear, in and of itself, can cause human beings to do things that are not in our best interests.

Why is that?

Fear attacks your sense of being in control, which can exacerbate other feelings such as uncertainty, worry, anxiety, and stress. When fear is in operation, it triggers the body's fight-or-flight system,[4] a very powerful and primitive impulse. Fear can also trigger what I call decision paralysis or the inability to make a decision.

This powerful human emotion is first felt in the region of the brain called the amygdala and triggers a release of stress hormones that can overwhelm the sympathetic nervous system.[5]

Most people are risk averse, particularly if the stakes are high or the terrain is unfamiliar. The reality is that selling your company does have risks and therefore triggers fears. The outcome of your sale is very important to you, and you probably have minimal, if any, experience in the legal, financial, and operational aspects of a sale.

But the risks in M&A are manageable. In fact, any intelligent M&A advisor knows what the risks are and manages them well in advance. The fact is, all of business boils down to assessing, accepting, and mitigating risk.

Think about it. When you opened your company, you were taking a risk that you could find clients, perform the services

---

3   "First Inaugural Address," fdrlibrary.org (FDR Presidential Library & Museum), accessed April 20, 2023, https://www.fdrlibrary.org/first-inaugural-curriculum-hub.

4   Ibid.

5   Arash Javanbakht and Linda Saab, "What Happens in the Brain When We Feel Fear," October 27, 2017, https://www.smithsonianmag.com/science-nature/what-happens-brain-feel-fear-180966992/.

required, and make a profit. Every time you hired an employee, bought expensive new equipment, or invested in R & D, you took a calculated risk. So let's take a hard look at some of the risks associated with selling your business.

- You are afraid you might not be able to sell. Reading this book will reduce this fear (i.e., de-risk) by helping you understand the characteristics of companies that are transferable and the characteristics of those that are not. If you understand this before going to market, you will be better prepared.

- You are afraid of selling at too low a price. Read on and we'll talk about how to determine a realistic value for your company before going to market. You will need to look at "market comps"—what similarly situated companies like yours have recently sold for. This knowledge will reduce your fear that you could end up selling too low.

- You are afraid that employees or customers might find out that you are selling. The risk of confidentiality being breached can be reduced by using a competent M&A advisor, using a measured process, and being sure you, the owner, don't spill the beans to the wrong person at the wrong time. That involves self-management, something you know how to do.

LOSS OF IDENTITY

When I founded my company, sbLiftOff, people asked me, "What does the 'sb' stand for?" I replied, "It stands for 'small business.'" But that wasn't the whole truth. The name of my company incorporates two of my own initials. I'm Sharon Beth Heaton. So the "sb" in my company name, "sbLiftOff," carries a special meaning for me and for people close to me.

Do I think my company is me? Of course not.

Just like you, I know that to have a successful company, it can't all be about me. You hired people, delegated tasks, and let go of responsibilities to scale. But even so, you no doubt have a core sense of identity connected to your company writ large. Even owners who have built companies worth hundreds of millions of dollars with thousands of employees have a sense of identity from owning their companies.

You are doubtless aware that when other people hear about your company, they immediately say, "Oh, that's so-and-so's company."

Like me, you have been to many business events, and someone has put a name tag on you that featured your name and the name of your company. When people ask what you do, you can answer with your title at your company.

Without you, America would not be the powerhouse it is today.

With the sale of your company, what goes on that name tag? How do you answer the question of what you do? These are normal questions that can trigger an existential crisis of identity. The sale of your business will force you to answer the question, "Who am I? Do I have any value on my own without running and owning my business?" It's worth thinking about this issue ahead of time so that you can answer those big life questions.

I have an answer that I'd like you to consider.

The American economy and the American people rely on business owners like you to create jobs and services and products. Without you and people like you who are brave enough and hardworking enough to build a profitable business, America would not be the economic powerhouse it is today. Of course, you have value in and of yourself. People like you who build profitable businesses across America are the backbone of the US economy.

You have done something few people are able to do. You were able to run and grow a profitable business. You have hired people and paid your taxes and persevered against all odds. This work of your life had a massive impact not just on you and your family but also on the lives of your employees and the larger community.

A business like yours is like throwing a pebble into a pond and seeing the ripple effects go and go and go. You have done a lot of good, and those ripple effects will continue even after you lift off from your business. On a core level, you should feel very confident that your life has great value and that you've created not just value but also much good.

Now you are moving on. You are entering a different part of your life. Just as there was a time in your life when you were single, a time in your life when you married, a time when you had children, a time after children—this is a new chapter of your life. The empty nesters who wave on the driveway as their children go off to college always remain parents. That part of your identity does not go away. But like those parents with older kids, you now will have time to nourish different parts of your identity and move on to the next chapter.

It's important to have a sense of what that next chapter in your identity might be. For example, I have a client who owned a logistics company. After selling his large and profitable logistics business, he now focuses on a charity that serves wounded veterans. This guy has his identity—and his next chapter of life—figured out.

Think about what you want to do next. Find something that you care about. Perhaps you want to devote more time to your family or pursue your passion for music. Whatever it is that you care about, do it. Don't stop growing and giving. Invest in the next phase of your life by charting a new path that you define, and take what you have learned as a business owner forward. You have gifts to share with the world.

FEELING JUDGED AND INADEQUATE

During the sale of your company, there will be strangers performing "due diligence." You *will* feel judged during the process! This is very common. You have been your own boss for years, and no one told you what to do, nor did people outside your business assess your performance.

I had a client who owned a healthy construction company that provided top-tier services while generating 12 percent net margins. As a family-owned business, they had developed their own accounting system that wasn't in compliance with Generally Accepted Accounting Principles (GAAP). When this was pointed out during due diligence, the client felt insulted. "Why do we have to do what everyone else does when we are making lots of money?" While his point was understandable, it was also understandable that buyers wanted to evaluate the company pursuant to GAAP.

Judging a company is not the same as judging the owner, and this is the type of assessment that will occur during due diligence. It can feel like you are getting a report card. People are doing an evaluation of your company, and they're going to assign a value to it, a grade if you will. I find business owners get nervous about that because they feel this is the ultimate report card based on something very concrete: money. You can easily feel judged, defensive, angry, or inadequate.

It is important to remember that a buyer is not judging you as a person. A buyer is sizing up your company. As the owner/seller, it's important to have some level of detachment and be able to differentiate between you and your worth as a human being and your company's worth at a moment in time in the market. Every company, no matter how wonderful, when it goes on the market will undergo due diligence. Don't take it personally!

Always keep this in mind and expect questions, and more questions, and more questions. Expect to have to share financial information. At the appropriate time, expect to share information about customers, employees, and other highly confidential data. To have a successful handoff to a new buyer, the other party must have detailed knowledge.

Don't let the feeling of being judged or feeling inadequate control you.

CONTROLLING THE "THREE HORSEMEN OF THE APOCALYPSE"

In his *Forbes* article titled "Emotional Control: The Hidden Secret to Business Success," Nicholas Earls, a certified emotional intelligence expert and coach, highlights the importance of managing emotions well. He notes, "Emotional intelligence is concerned with your ability to manage your own emotions, as well as how well you perceive and interact with the emotions of others."[6]

Years ago I was finishing a meeting with a new client who was bringing his company to market. "Well," he said, "I'm convinced you can handle the M&A transaction. But what are you going to do to preserve my mental health?"

I laughed then told him, "I definitely see that as one of my jobs. I'm going to keep you informed, which will reduce your fear. We're going to talk about what to do after you sell your company to confront your identity issues. And I'm going to remind you that your company is being evaluated, not you personally."

---

6   Nicholas Earls, "Emotional Control: The Hidden Secret to Business Success," July 26, 2022, https://www.forbes.com/sites/forbesbusinesscouncil/2022/07/26/emotional-control-the-hidden-secret-to-business-success/?sh=26a2600f1e94.

The sale of your company probably represents the single largest financial transaction of your lifetime. That's a big deal that will constantly knock on your emotional door. But don't let those big emotions of fear and uncertainty, loss of identity, and feeling judged or inadequate obscure an extremely relevant fact: on the other side of the sale, you are monetizing your life's work.

If you can acknowledge the Three Horsemen of the Apocalypse, understand what's ahead, and remain objective, you will be able to manage your M&A journey with emotional hygiene.

Success will enable you to lift off to your next adventure in life!

LIFT OFF LESSONS

- Selling your business is not just a financial transaction; it's also a highly emotional transaction that carries challenges.
- Take note of the emotions you feel about selling your business and explore them, but don't be controlled by them.
- Feelings of fear and uncertainty, loss of identity, and feeling judged and inadequate are common and normal. Don't let emotions get in the way of planning for the sale of your company.
- Think about the next challenge you want to take on after you sell your business. This is an opportunity to reimagine yourself and your life. What's next on your bucket list?
- Be intelligent, be informed, act sensibly, and don't overreact. Recognize that while you will have strong feelings, you want to manage this transaction rationally.

CHAPTER 2

WHAT'S THE SECRET TO A SUCCESSFUL DEAL?

After all my years of dealmaking, I am often asked, "What is the secret to a successful deal?"

My answer will surprise you.

It's not about killer instinct or being smarter than other people. It's not even about the megatrends going on in the market.

The secret to a successful deal is to be able to see everything from the other person's perspective. If there's a superpower in M&A, it is *empathy*. Why empathy? Because it will allow you to understand the other party's goals, sensitivities, and perspectives.

The dictionary definition of empathy is "the action of understanding, being aware of, being sensitive to, and vicariously experiencing the feelings, thoughts, and experience of another" person. It is the understanding "of either the past or present without having the feelings, thoughts, and experience fully communicated in an objectively explicit manner."

Imagine the insight you would have prior to a deal negotiation if you understood with perfect clarity the other side's feelings, thoughts, and perspective, the other party's past and present experiences that led them to a deal with you. That would be amazing, right?

To have a successful M&A transaction between seller and buyer, it is essential that the deal stays on track and that you can see down the road to any potential bumps. Empathy will give you that visibility; it's almost like a navigation system. Naturally, with the pressure of a large sum hanging over your head and the sale of your business in the future, you're going to be very focused on your own feelings and objectives during the transaction. That's normal but also a big mistake. Good deals must be good for *both* parties. The more the buyer and the seller understand what's important to the other person—not just the numbers but many other issues as well—the more likely the deal will be to close.

Empathy allows both parties to see the selling of a company as more than a simple transaction. Empathizing with the other person brings the "human" element of buying and selling into focus, and that human element is crucial.

A WIN-WIN PARTNERSHIP

The sale of your business is a life-changing transaction and is, in essence, a partnership. The buyer and the seller are tied together through a challenging period of time and must work together to get the deal done. Regardless of whether the business is worth $3 million or $30 million, getting the right deal done is a gargantuan task taking many hours, many concessions, and many meetings.

When all is said and done, the goal is to have a successful handoff of your company. In many ways you are passing a golden baton, one that cannot drop to the ground. It cannot break. The handoff must be smooth. For this to happen, the transaction should not be an adversarial relationship. If it becomes ugly and contentious, the conditions will be less than ideal when it comes to a smooth handoff.

Sometimes buyers can be dismissive and rude toward sellers, essentially lacking empathy. It's never a good thing for a buyer to introduce themselves that way. Similarly, I've witnessed sellers being childish, petty, and self-centered. In short, lacking empathy for the buyer's feelings.

> **The best way to build a win-win partnership is for buyers to think like sellers and sellers to think like buyers.**

M&A professionals who work in the midmarket recognize that there should be no absolute winners or losers. M&A is a team sport, and both parties should win. The best way to build a win-win partnership is for buyers to think like sellers and sellers to think like buyers, and that takes empathy.

ISSUES THAT BUYERS NEED TO HAVE EMPATHY TOWARD

The buyer must recognize the personal investment that you, the founder/owner, have in your company. That is something separate from your financial requirements and is part of the emotional transaction I've mentioned. In fact, the sale of your company is a life transition, not a simple transaction.

Every founder/owner has many issues on the table, including the future for their employees. You probably care as much about what happens to your people as you do about the final selling price of your company. You also want to be reassured that the buyer you select will respect your employees. You'll also care about your company's legacy, particularly how your buyer will maintain your company's reputation with other business partners and customers.

It's normal for an owner of a company to care what happens to your business years from now, and you want to probe a buyer's reason for purchasing your company.

Any reputable buyer should be prepared to answer the following questions:

- What are your long-term plans to grow my company once transferred?
- Where are you getting your financing?
- What are your plans for the employees?
- How certain can I be that this deal will close?

This final question is perhaps the biggest concern sellers have, and any smart buyer understands this.

ISSUES THAT SELLERS NEED TO HAVE EMPATHY ABOUT

As nervous as sellers are, buyers are often even more nervous—and with good reason. On the day of closing, the seller will always know more about the company than the buyer, regardless of the level of due diligence the buyer has done. The seller needs empathy toward the buyer, understanding that the buyer is making a major financial decision with incomplete information. Sellers can show empathy and respect by being transparent and open and assisting the buyer in learning about the company.

WHY LYING AND OBFUSCATION ARE STUPID

It's possible that you are saying, "Why do I have to care about this other person? I'm sick of being Mr. Nice Guy. I'm going to do whatever I have to do to get the price I want for my company!"

Good luck with that approach because you'll find that lying and obfuscation always backfire. Acting with integrity is the best path to closing a deal.

To state the obvious, your company, like all companies, has strengths and weaknesses. As you go to market, it is far better to be up front about both. Do not let the "sales" process get in the way of accurately describing your company because the truth will come out. For example, as the seller, you don't want to paint a rosy picture about sales forecasts to your buyer and then have that person find out that your company doesn't have the inventory to match. And you certainly don't want to talk about cash on hand without stating that your company is behind in payments to various vendors.

It is imperative that your company's strengths and challenges be presented to your buyer honestly before you reach a commercial understanding, which is memorialized in the LOI. The LOI must be based on the reality of what your company truly is and isn't. As we will discuss later, after the LOI is signed, intensive due diligence begins. If you've been open and transparent, then due diligence will be confirmatory in nature. You will establish trust between the parties. If, however, you have been hiding challenges, the next stage will be painful.

The letter of intent should have baked into it the true strengths and weaknesses of your company. After the LOI is signed, due diligence should be *confirmatory*. In other words, the buyer should be able to verify that everything you told them was true. When buyers find out things that you haven't told them, that's not good for you, and it's not good for the deal. Honesty, really, is the best policy.

Let's play that out and assume there is some litigation risk, or employee disputes, or a tax issue that has not been disclosed to the buyer before the LOI. The buyer is highly likely to find the undisclosed issue during the post LOI and due diligence process. The buyer will then think that either the seller did not know about the problem, making the buyer very nervous, or the seller knew about the problem and did not disclose it, which destroys trust.

At this point either the buyer walks away from the deal entirely, or they ask for the dreaded price adjustment. This is something that you, the owner and seller of a business, want to avoid at all costs! It's normal to be reluctant to put a negative light on your company and to fear full disclosure. But it's imperative that you look at your company from the buyer's point of view and understand that full disclosure is the best approach.

Put yourself in your buyer's shoes.

What would you want to know about products, services, inventory, employee retention, EBITDA, net earnings, and other facets of the business if you were buying your company? How would you want someone to treat you? What level of honesty and transparency would you expect?

CULTURAL LITERACY AND EMPATHY

I once wrote an article in *Harvard Business Review* about something I called "cultural literacy." Cultural literacy is understanding the values, the words, the language, and the assumptions that a group other than your own holds dear. In fact, this is nothing more than having empathy for a group of people. Many times, middle-market business owners do not live in the same culture as their buyers. That can cause disagreements and misunderstandings.

A study from the National Center for the Middle Market found that 90 percent of middle-market owners who sell or merge have "little or no previous experience" in M&A.[7] In contrast, many buyers, especially large strategics or private equity (PE) players, are full-time M&A professionals. These professional buyers often hail from urban areas and elite universities. They often view business deals as financial transactions only and have no emotional connections to them. These individuals can be quite analytical and dispassionate in their approach.

Many professional buyers conduct multiple transactions every year and have a lot of pressure to deploy capital. They usually have masters they are serving and are on a short-time leash. They might also carry themselves with a master-of-the-universe air, knowing that they have millions at their disposal. However, none of that gives license to be offensive or tone-deaf to founders and owners of thriving businesses. You, and countless others like you, have done something exceptional: you've built a cash-generating machine. Professional buyers value that cash-generating machine, yet sometimes, despite their best efforts, they can be tone-deaf and culturally obtuse, refusing to see or recognize the importance of that very feat.

---

7   National Center for the Middle Market, "Middle Market M&A," accessed October 3, 2022, https://www.middlemarketcenter.org/Media/Documents/key-findings-middle-market-merger-and-acqusition-best-practices-key-findings.pdf.

The founder/owner and a PE buyer may also use a very different "business speak"—terms of reference, code words, and jokes known to insiders.

I recall one PE buyer with an advanced degree from Oxford. He had completed scores of M&A transactions and originally hailed from Belgium. My client was selling his large and very profitable national US company but did not have a college degree. These two barely understood each other's words, sentences, and worlds, and I was thrust into the role of translator.

Cultural literacy is understanding the other person's lingo, the other person's world. My client was not a finance brainiac with an advanced degree from Oxford. He had never been to Belgium and did not have a pied-à-terre[8] in New York City. These two individuals were not better or worse than the other, just different.

If you start having trouble communicating with your buyer—not understanding words, acronyms, or phrases or feeling an uncomfortable sense of alienation or cultural disconnect—don't be surprised. This happens often and can be mitigated. Having empathy for the other party is the solution, as well as having experienced professionals in your corner who can translate. A win-win mindset and a healthy helping of empathy go a long way to focus everyone on overcoming all impediments and getting to the close. That, in short, is the secret to a successful deal.

---

8   A small apartment, house, or room kept for occasional use.

LIFT OFF LESSONS

- The secret to a successful closed deal is having empathy— putting yourself in the other party's shoes.
- Successful buyers and sellers look at the company from each other's point of view and understand what is important to the other party.
- Buyers should be prepared to explain their plans for the business, their financing sources, their plans for the employees, and the certainty that they can close.
- Sellers should recognize that buyers are taking on a risk and need to do extensive due diligence to satisfy themselves that the deal will be a good one.
- Founders/owners need and deserve respect from buyers— respect for the key employees, the company's legacy, and the company's reputation with other business partners and customers alike.
- Buyers want respect through transparent and open communi- cation as they learn about the company they are buying.

CHAPTER 3

HOW DO I MAINTAIN CONFIDENTIALITY?

Every business owner I speak with is concerned about maintaining confidentiality—and rightly so! They don't want people to know that they are selling their company.

As the owner of your company, you owe it to yourself to keep the sale confidential, meaning you only take into your confidence those who truly need to know. It is not in your best interests—or in the best interests of the sale of your company—to tell employees, suppliers, or customers or competitors too early in the process. Even rumors of a potential sale can be destabilizing.

The following are good reasons to keep things confidential:

- Change makes employees nervous. News of a potential sale can quickly create unrest. "Who will buy the company?" "What will the company look like going forward?" and the all-important "Will I still have my job when ownership changes hands?"

Worries like this are fodder for watercooler or Slack discussions. Employees can quickly get caught up in the unknowns, which can affect job performance. To maintain a stable workforce, limit the number of people who know about the sale of your company until the time is right to tell everyone.

- Competitors can use information about your potential sale to your disadvantage. They might poach employees: "You better jump ship so that you don't lose your job." They may tell customers that they cannot rely on your company or you: "Did you know that one company is for sale? Who knows what the new owners will be like? However, what we can offer you is …"

- If word of the sale of your company gets out before you are fully prepared, you may lose new or long-standing contracts. Suppliers and customers alike want to know there is long-term stability, and both may be hesitant if they know that a sale is imminent.

Most owners know intuitively that confidentiality is crucial to a successful sale. Those who do not end up broadcasting their inner dialogue of "Shall I sell, or shall I not sell?" with other stakeholders, which is rarely a good idea.

At the same time, it is not possible to market or sell anything, including your firm, without talking to people. So let's take a look at that.

When you sell a house, an important financial asset that also has emotional value to you, you can put a big For Sale sign out front, along with print advertisements and digital listings. The idea is to tell as many people as possible so that all the potential buyers will vie for your home, allowing you to get the best price.

Even with the openness of this process, over 90 percent of home-owners retain a real estate agent.[9] The reason? It is generally under-stood that selling a house also requires both time and marketing skills, and it makes the most sense for a homeowner to delegate the task to an expert who has experience and can do a better job.

Selling your company is a lot more complicated than selling your home.

Because of the need for confidentiality, there can be no sign out front promoting a sale, there can be no advertisements, and you cannot discuss strategy, valuation, or potential buyers with internal parties. As a result, if you care about confidentiality, one of the first realizations you will come to is the need to hire an M&A advisor.

If you try to sell your company yourself, your options are limited. You can contact your lawyer, your accountant, and maybe your commercial banker to let them know you are looking for a buyer. You can instruct these people to keep the name of your company confidential and to let you know if anyone is interested. Some business owners try to do that, but the likelihood of success is small. Lawyers, accountants, and bankers, however well networked, are not in the daily business of selling companies. Their universe may be big, but it probably does not encompass all possible buyers, not just in your state but also across the country and the world.

If you try to sell your company yourself, your options are limited.

I had a client based in a small community in Maryland, serving the United States, whose company became of great interest to a global

---

9   National Association of Realtors, "Quick Real Estate Statistics," November 3, 2022, https://www.nar.realtor/research-and-statistics/quick-real-estate-statistics.

company based in England trying to expand into the US market. You never know where that best buyer will come from.

Sometimes business owners decide they're just going to sell their company themselves. This is a very dangerous approach. Business owners who market their company themselves forfeit confidentiality and feed the rumor mill. This makes you *and* your company vulnerable.

A brilliant client came to me a few years ago. She had a PhD in astrophysics and had built an innovative health IT company. She wanted to sell her company and wanted to do it quickly and inexpensively. So she picked up the phone and talked to the owners of the three other large companies in her field that she knew would have a strategic interest in buying her company.

What was the result?

Not only did the other companies tell everyone inside the industry that she was eager to sell, but they also poached her key employees and provided her with offers—letters of intent—at pennies on the dollar of what her company was worth. By the time she came to me, two years had passed. The contracts coming into her company had declined, the strength of her employee base had weakened, and she now had far fewer options in terms of selling her company. She has been her own worst enemy. Her methodology was not inexpensive and certainly not fast.

Think hard and long before you try to sell your company yourself. One of the consequences of doing so is forfeiting confidentiality.

HOW A PROFESSIONAL M&A ADVISOR PROTECTS YOUR CONFIDENTIALITY

An M&A advisor uses several tools and processes to protect your confidentiality. It is best described as a "gating" process. The seller and the buyer open one gate at a time, and the next gate isn't opened until both parties agree. Information is only shared that is appropriate for each gate.

BLIND TEASER

A "blind teaser" provides high-level information about a company for sale without identifying the company's name. It's important that this blind teaser doesn't give away the true identity of the company. For example, if you were to copy information in the teaser and put it into Google, the name of the company should not come up.

A blind teaser should be high level enough to help a potential buyer determine if they have an interest. For instance, HVAC versus IT, mid-Atlantic as opposed to Tennessee, or one hundred or one thousand employees.

Specific information should be included, such as revenues in round numbers over the last several years and projections for the next few years. A potential buyer needs to understand if this is a $10 million revenue company or a $40 million revenue company. Some information about margins is often included because margins can determine a buyer's level of interest. Some buyers will not consider companies with less than a certain margin, while others might be looking for a company with lower margins that can be optimized.

Here are a couple of things to note about the teaser:

- Limit the number of recipients to fifty or fewer. In prior years, the teaser was sent out to hundreds of potential buyers. Today the number is more targeted.
- Remember the purpose of the teaser. After it is sent, you want to find out who will raise their hand and say, "I'm interested, and I'd like to know more."
- Be sure to construct it in a way that helps you narrow the field of potential buyers based on your selling criteria.

Blind teasers include information on what you, the owner, want potential buyers to know about your goals: sale of 100 percent, sale of minority interest, and other considerations.

After receiving the blind teaser, some potential buyers will indicate interest in learning more. They will not be replying to you and will be contacting the M&A advisor, whom they know represents a plethora of sellers.

Before giving out any further information, the M&A advisor should share the identity of any potential buyers interested in receiving more information. You may know the potential buyer and see them as a direct competitor or an unworthy successor to your company.

NONDISCLOSURE AGREEMENT

If you are ready to move ahead, your M&A advisor will have the prospective buyer or buyers sign a nondisclosure agreement, or NDA. As M&A advisors, we have potential buyers sign an NDA with us on behalf of our client. The potential buyer only learns of the name of the selling company *after* the NDA is signed.

Without an M&A advisor, the document is directly exchanged between the buyer and the seller. In that instance, the buyer learns the identity of the seller without signing an NDA. This is a mistake and would ultimately leave the seller exposed.

CONFIDENTIAL INFORMATION MEMORANDUM

After the NDA is signed, a third document called a confidential information memorandum (CIM) comes into play. This is a standard document that provides more information about the seller, including the identity of the seller and some high-level information, but not important competitive information. This is an initial, but not total, reveal of top-level information about your business.

A good M&A advisor knows how to manage the information flow without giving away too many facts during this stage. This is an individualized process that takes some discernment and judgment.

Additionally, do not make the mistake of believing all your information is sensitive. This is an error that many sellers make. For instance, an organizational chart can be useful to a buyer to understand how your business operates. It is not a good idea, however, to put the names of your employees on this chart.

One way that you and your M&A advisor will make the decision to go forward and share more information with a potential buyer is by doing some due diligence on them, which I'll go into more detail in chapter 10. You need to be fully satisfied that any potential buyer is indeed a credible buyer.

This brings us to a topic that isn't well understood by nonprofessionals: there are a lot of tire kickers out there.

Why, you ask, would someone pretend to be a buyer but in truth is not?

There are many answers to that question, but the fact is that tire kickers exist and are a genuine nuisance. They might be

- competitors seeking information,
- people who want to know what is going on in the market and willingly sign many NDAs in order to educate themselves, or
- people who suffer from big-man-on-campus syndrome and like the feeling of acting as if they can purchase a multimillion-dollar revenue company but in reality cannot.

None of the above people are individuals who should have access to your data.

Only after the teaser, the NDA, research on the buyer, and the buyer's indication of interest in moving ahead are in place, only then is the "data room" made available. The data room contains more detailed information about your company.

There is a difference of opinion on the next step.

Some sellers want to get a buyer to offer an LOI as quickly as possible. The seller's rationale is that the buyer can do more due diligence after the LOI is signed.

I disagree.

The buyer should be encouraged—and even required—to do serious due diligence on the seller prior to an LOI to ensure that the buyer understands the strengths and challenges of the selling entity. Despite this need for more due diligence, prior to the signing of an LOI, some information, such as a list of the names of employees, can be withheld until after the LOI.

Be aware there is a constant tension between what should be disclosed and when throughout the process. This is normal.

The seller must disclose enough information to allow the buyer to determine their level of interest and what they feel is an appropriate valuation for the company while protecting truly confidential information. Confidentiality should be protected not just by you and your M&A advisor but also by all your professional advisors and those close to you—your lawyer, accountant, and any close confidants, such as your spouse, life partner, child, or key employee.

Now here is a reality.

While you may still feel like you are forty years old, the truth may be that you are in your late fifties or older. Even if other people do not know that you are thinking about transferring your company, many people will *assume* that you are or at least considering it simply because of your age. It is possible there may be rumors, so don't be surprised if there are. Just follow best practice and protect confidentiality, and the likelihood of your transaction will increase.

LIFT OFF LESSONS

- It is never in your best interests—or in the best interests of the sale of your company—to tell your employees, your suppliers, or your customers too early in the process.
- If you try to sell your business yourself, your options are severely limited. One of the consequences is forfeiting confidentiality.
- A "teaser" is the first sales document. It introduces the opportunity to purchase but cannot be tied to your company, protecting confidentiality.
- An NDA is essential to have with any potential buyer.
- Vetted buyers receive a CIM, which provides more detailed information about your company.
- These standard M&A documents act as a "gateway" to determine when to disclose information, how, and to whom. They're important to get right.

CHAPTER 4

IS MY COMPANY SELLABLE?

I was in a meeting with an owner of a food services company. The company prepared meals and delivered them around the country. While sitting at a table with my client, during our ninety-minute conversation, several of his employees called with questions such as "The sink is stopped up. Who should we call?" "Mary didn't show up at work today. What should we do?" "The invoice is missing. Where do we look?"

I knew that the company had been operating at a profit for years but was aghast to realize that the employees had no idea how to run the company without the owner's input and direction. This owner didn't have a company. He had a job with staff. His employees were a labor force multiplier. They were helping him do his job, and they weren't doing their own jobs.

At the end of the meeting, I said to him, "I'm not sure that your company is transferable. How will the business continue to perform after you're gone?"

He looked at me and said, "Well, somebody would need to play my role."

I replied, "You're working ninety hours a week. No one else is going to do that. We need to restructure your company so that you have a defined role. If you were removed, someone else could step in. Your employees also need to have full responsibility for their jobs without getting continual day-to-day direction from you."

As the founder/owner of your company, you must ask yourself a very important question: Are you running your business 24/7, or are there people within your company who can maintain company operations if you weren't there?

Your answer to this question will determine if you have a company that's sellable or if you have a job with a staff reporting to you. Another way I ask owners this question is, "If you walked into the parking lot and got struck by lightning today, what would happen to your company tomorrow?"

Potential buyers want to know that your company will continue its operations without you being there.

If you begin to panic because you have no idea what would happen, you have some work to do in order to make your company sellable.

Potential buyers want to know that your company will continue its operations without you being there. When a buyer puts lots of money into the pocket of the seller, the buyer questions whether the seller will work as hard after the transaction as before.

Moreover, the transition from entrepreneur to employee is challenging. The buyer wants to know that the company has a stable and responsible workforce with people who will work independently of the seller. In the buyer's eyes, this is critical knowledge, giving them reassurance as to the ongoing feasibility of the company.

THE VALUE OF THE MACHINE

My response to the question, "Is my company sellable?" is to ask another question: "Is the machine itself useful and, if so, to whom?"

For example, this might seem counterintuitive, but in some respects, a cardboard box manufacturer might be far more valuable than a high-end law firm. Here's a comparison between the two companies.

The high-end law firm might have three lawyers, each of whom earns millions of dollars a year. The cardboard manufacturer might have twenty employees not earning nearly as much. To make the point clearer, let's assume the revenue and profit of the law firm are higher. In most cases the cardboard box manufacturer will have a buyer willing to pay more cash at close than a buyer for the law firm.

When a client retains a law firm, they specifically want to hire a specific lawyer. If that lawyer is unavailable, the client might look for a different law firm. If a lawyer leaves that firm, all the clients might move with that individual to a new law firm.

When a customer goes to the cardboard box manufacturer, they don't care who does the work; they simply want to get their order of cardboard boxes filled. Further, if the ownership of the cardboard box company changed hands, customers wouldn't care so long as the assembly line continued its day-to-day operations. The cardboard box company can easily be valued based upon its financial performance; it can be transferred without a loss of revenue or profit. High-end service companies such as this law firm may actually have lower valuations than a manufacturing company because of ownership involvement and not because of the goods and services being produced.

In the case of the law firm, it's easy to think that lawyers are interchangeable the same way that pens are interchangeable. But the firm's clients certainly wouldn't think that way, and neither should potential buyers of that firm.

The issue is whether the company can continue to provide its goods and services to clients at the same quality and be able to attract new business to the company if the ownership wasn't there. Buyers will often look to see who is managing the company other than the owners.

If it's only the owners, then it's very questionable as to whether or not that engine is transferable.

If, in fact, employees who are not owners are deeply involved in running the company, the engine itself has more value. It's a little bit of a dichotomy that buyers want the owner to be less important. And sometimes owners make themselves more important, thinking that they're doing the right thing when, in fact, they're undermining the value of their company.

THE IMPORTANCE OF MANAGEMENT

If a business is a machine, then management is the engine. The engine is what drives the machine, so the machine is only as strong as the engine.

A buyer will want to know if the current management will continue "driving the business" by providing the same level of expertise and proficiency after the sale as before. The buyer wants to know that your company will continue to provide its goods and services to clients with the same quality and be able to attract new business.

I worked with a high-end IT company, owned by Jack and Patricia, doing digital transformation work for its customers. They had incredibly impressive backgrounds, and for the first two years, they served as subject matter experts who serviced clients directly.

Jack and Patricia were smart. They knew early on that their ultimate goal was to sell their company. They understood that to sell, the company had to have employees who were the subject matter experts, other employees who managed the day-to-day operations of the company, and customer relationships that were distributed throughout the employees.

Over the next six years, they hired and trained employees and put an organizational structure in place. The organization chart showed the two of them at the top, but every other function of the company was handled by their employees. Eventually, they passed the "litmus test" regarding whether or not a company can function independent of ownership.

First, Jack went on vacation for two weeks. All was well. He came back, and soon after Patricia went on vacation. Again, all was well. Finally, both of them went on vacation at the same time for one week. They were as nervous as a parent sitting in the passenger seat while their teenager drives a car for the first time.

It worked!

The company operated without them. Employees brought in a new client, and work was delivered on existing projects. We knew that the company was sellable.

The good news: we had a great response from the market!

POLICIES AND PROCEDURES

One of the hallmarks of a company that is transferable is having written policies and procedures (P&P). These P&P serve as a manual that details and regulates all major decisions, actions, and business principles of your company. The manual contains documents that provide authority and necessary direction for your company and/or a department on topics such as hiring practices, bank accounts, dress code (or lack thereof), what to do in an emergency, and much more.

In my initial meeting with clients, I always ask this question: "Are your company's policies and procedures all in your head, or are they written down?"

Even if a company has a strong management team, if only one person, including the owner, has the P&P in their head and leaves the company, that single point of failure will diminish the value of the company at the time of sale.

As the owner/founder, you want to make sure that you are not the only person who knows the P&P. All company employees need to understand what their job is, what they are responsible for doing, and what the available tools are for them to accomplish their responsibilities. There should be job descriptions for every position.

P&P ensure that the company acts in the same way under similar circumstances so that it is not constantly reinventing the wheel.

If a sales approach worked well, write it down.

If a problem arises with a client and is resolved well, write it down.

In fact, if steps are taken that don't work out, write that down as well. Don't make the same mistakes again.

P&P give a buyer comfort that the business will continue to operate in the same way once you are no longer the owner.

Everything about your company needs to be written down to avoid ad hoc decision-making and company lore through hearsay. A business that doesn't have continuity and consistency has less value and in the worst situations might not be transferable at all.

CUSTOMER RELATIONSHIPS

Going back to my definition of a company as something that takes in revenue and throws out profit, the revenue that comes into the company is the result of one thing: customers. To simplify this further, "No customers, no business."

I worked with a manufacturing firm in the aerospace industry. The owner had set up the company so that it would continue manufacturing parts if he wasn't there.

Excellent!

However, the owner was the only person in touch with the clients, and he jealously guarded those relationships. In fact, he was the single point of contact for all customers. Upon realizing this, I looked him straight in the eye and said, "The company may run without you, but where is future business going to come from if you aren't there?"

We had further discussions about this, and over the next year, he started introducing other people in their organization to all clients and giving the clients more points of contact within the company.

When a problem came up and an employee brought it to the owner, he said, "Call the client yourself and resolve the issue. I'm here to help if you need it, but you can do it."

By the end of the second year, customer-employee relationship connections were embedded throughout the company, and the company was now sellable.

When you're ready to sell your company, you want to be sure the company is *truly* ready to sell.

LIFT OFF LESSONS

- A business is like a "machine" that spins out profits. In order to be sellable, that machine needs to create profit if you, the founder/owner, are no longer associated with it.

- The question you need to ask is, can this "machine" of yours provide its goods or services to clients at the same quality and be able to attract new business to the company without you? If so, your company is sellable.

- A company's P&P serve as a manual that details and regulates all major decisions, actions, and business principles of a company. Do you have this type of manual?

- Customer relations are key to a sale, and those relationships must go beyond just you. Can your business keep and serve customers should ownership change hands?

CHAPTER 5

HOW DO I GET PAID?

When you sell your home, in most circumstances, the purchaser pays 100 percent cash at closing, and the seller drops the keys on the table and walks away. That rarely is how privately held companies sell.

The following are four ways sellers get paid for their companies:

1. Cash at close
2. Seller financing
3. Equity rollover
4. Earnout

CASH AT CLOSE

The simplest method for sellers to get paid is cash at close. While sellers want as much cash at close, buyers often want to minimize that same cash. Depending upon the transaction, sellers should expect somewhere between 50 and 80 percent of the value paid in cash at close. This is a heavily negotiated point.

This leads to the obvious question: Why doesn't the seller get the full value in cash at close?

There are two main reasons. First, on the day of close, the seller will always know more about the company than the buyer, regardless of how much due diligence the buyer has done. So as nervous as the seller is about the transaction, the buyer is even more nervous. The buyer's concern is that the seller knows of problems that the buyer has not yet discovered. The buyer is trying to "read" the intent of the seller. If the seller wants 100 percent of the value of the company in cash at close, the buyer's nervousness increases (i.e., why doesn't the seller believe that their company will be able to pay the additional sum?).

Second, to achieve a purchase price satisfactory to both the buyer and the seller, the buyer may want the seller to share in some future risk. These transactions are called "structured" and usually result in a higher purchase price, with some risk sharing between the buyer and the seller.

Payment of purchase price can be structured using the remaining tools for compensating sellers.

SELLER FINANCING

When the buyer and the seller agree that some portion of the purchase price will be paid to the seller over time, the term that is used is "seller financing." For instance, let's assume that the purchase price is $10 million, and the buyer can only pay $8 million cash at close. The seller can "finance" the remaining $2 million in purchase price with the buyer paying this amount over the next several years.

There are some important things to know about seller financing.

It is not contingent; the buyer *owes* the seller these funds. The company does not need to achieve certain milestones for the buyer to be obligated to pay the seller financing. However, seller financing is guaranteed by the company being transferred, not the buyer. Sellers always want—and I have never seen—a buyer provide a personal guarantee on this financing. So the risk to the seller is that the buyer will devalue the company such that there will not be funds to repay the seller. In other words, while seller financing is not contingent, it will not be paid if the company fails. This is less of a risk than you would think. The buyer in the above example has invested $8 million in the company. No one wants to lose their $8 million to avoid paying the seller the $2 million. Basically, the buyer has more to lose than the seller.

Seller financing is always subordinate to bank financing. Again, in the example above, $8 million is being paid at close, with $2 million in equity from the buyer and $6 million being borrowed from a bank. The bank will have a prior claim to get its $6 million repaid, and if the bank is not getting their payments, the seller will not receive their payments. The terms of the seller financing subordination to senior bank debt are carefully negotiated. In some circumstances, no payments are made on seller financing until the bank debt has been paid off. More commonly, sellers receive interest-only payments on their financing for an initial period, with principal starting to get paid at year two or three. Sometimes, the bank and the seller begin receiving principal and interest payments soon after the transaction.

There is a surprising side benefit to seller financing. As will be discussed later, in most transactions, the purchase agreement requires the seller to put 10–20 percent of the purchase price in an escrow for up to two years to protect the buyer from breaches of the representations and warranties made by the seller. If the transaction involves seller financing, the parties may agree to use the seller financing to protect the buyer, and the escrow can be eliminated.

EQUITY ROLLOVER

Equity rollover is another way sellers get "paid" for their company. In this situation, the seller retains some ownership in the company after the transaction. Returning to our previous example of the $10 million transaction with $8 million cash at close, the seller could retain 20 percent ownership after the transaction. Under this scenario, since the buyer is only acquiring 80 percent of a $10 million company, the seller has received all the value at close (80 percent in cash, the remaining value in rollover equity).

As with seller financing, equity rollover is not "contingent"; the seller owns this interest regardless of the success of the company. However, as with seller financing, if the company ultimately fails, the equity interest can lose its value. Again, the buyer wants to avoid this result, as they own an even greater percentage (in most circumstances) of the company. So the risk to the seller is less than the risk to the buyer.

Rollover equity can serve several purposes. As discussed above, at close, sellers will always know more about the company than the buyer. From the buyer's perspective, if the company is as terrific as the seller asserts, shouldn't the seller want to share in future growth? Therefore, sellers who are completely opposed to either seller financing or equity rollover can raise alarm bells for buyers. The buyer will ask, "Why doesn't the seller believe in the future of the company?"

Equity rollover can make a transaction more affordable for the buyer. For example, maybe the buyer cannot fund 100 percent of the purchase price of the company. An equity rollover can help bridge a financing gap for the buyer.

Perhaps the most important thing to know is this: equity rollovers can also be extremely lucrative for the seller. If you chose a buyer who is successful in growing your company, a second sale of the company might provide you with as much value as the initial sale.

In my years of doing transactions, I have seen equity rollovers have terrific results for clients.

For example, Sam and Martha had a managed service provider company they wanted to sell. We determined that their company was worth $17–$20 million. We went through the process and concluded a transaction with a $21 million purchase price, but the buyer wanted the seller to roll over 25 percent in equity. Sam and Martha were extremely hesitant but calculated that the $15.75 million[10] would meet their financial needs and were willing to "roll the dice" with the equity rollover. Sam and Martha stayed engaged in the company for a couple of years and then retired. Five years after Sam and Martha originally sold their company, the buyer sold the company again, except that the sales price was $100 million. At the time of the sale, the company had $20 million in debt that had to be paid off at close. Therefore, total proceeds to the owners were $80 million, with Sam and Martha selling their 25 percent for $20 million. They made more money on their sale of 25 percent than they did on the initial 75 percent sale!

It doesn't always work out this well, but this happens frequently, and it's worth considering.

EARNOUT

The fourth payment structure is an "earnout"—the dreaded earnout. Earnouts have a terrible reputation among business owners because, historically, they have been poorly structured. Of all issues in an M&A transaction, the earnout component is the most likely to lead to a

---

10   In this case, the seller's equity was valued at the purchase price. In some circumstances, particularly when the buyer is private equity, the seller can get their equity values "pari passu" with the buyer. In these situations, debt is not included in the valuation of the equity.

dispute and even litigation between the buyer and the seller after closing.

However, earnouts can play a very important role in bridging valuation disagreements between buyers and sellers.

Unlike seller financing and equity rollover, earnouts *are* contingent; the buyer only owes money to the seller if certain events specified between the parties occur after the closing. Why would a buyer be willing to pay the seller more for events that occur after closing? Why would a seller be willing to defer value for events that occur when they no longer control the company?

Business owners are like farmers, constantly planting seeds that are expected to turn into new opportunities, produce revenue, and increase profits. Sellers often want to not only get paid for the seeds that have flourished and are currently yielding profit but also compensated for the opportunities that they believe will occur. It is part of the value of their company.

Buyers will value the company as it exists at closing, rarely persuaded by the seller's coming attractions. Buyers pay for the *past*, but their decision to buy is based upon the *future*, hoping that those planted seeds sprout.

And what if the seeds never sprout? The buyer does not want to pay for something that might not occur but is probably willing to pay the seller more if it does.

Earnouts bridge this perspective gap between buyers and sellers.

Ann owned a $10 million revenue producing $2 million in EBITDA in the last calendar year. The company was growing rapidly and expecting $25 million in revenue for the current calendar year with $5 million in EBITDA. It was April, and revenue was rapidly increasing. If the first quarter's revenue held up for the next nine months, $25 million in revenue was realistic. The company's rapid growth was attractive to buyers; in fact, it was a significant reason that buyers were interested.

Ann said, "I want a five multiple based on what I expect the EBITDA to be this current year. Five times five is twenty-five."

Craig, a potential buyer, countered with "I will pay you for what has happened. The last fiscal year, you had $10 million in revenue and $2 million in EBITDA. If we look at the result from the trailing twelve months [so the strong first quarter is counted in favor of the seller], revenue was $16 million with EBITDA of $3.2 million. I am willing to pay five times 3.2 for a $16 million purchase price."

In summary, Ann wanted to be paid for the future, while Craig was only willing to pay for the past, even though his interest was based upon the projected rapid growth. This illustrates the biggest difference between the perspectives of buyers and sellers, and this is where an earnout comes into play.

Craig would be willing to pay $25 million if there were $5 million in EBITDA but does not want to pay for EBITDA that might not happen. Ann wanted to be paid $25 million because she was so certain EBITDA would be $5 million.

Ann and Craig came to an agreement. They would close the transaction and base the payment at close on five times the EBITDA from the trailing twelve months. And for the twelve months postclosing, further purchase price would be paid by Craig to Ann based upon agreed-upon financial targets. Over time Ann received her $25 million.

Here is another example.

Seth and Harold were selling their forty-year-old modestly profitable environmental consulting company, with margins ranging from 3 to 9 percent. Seth was particularly excited because their firm had just landed a new contract with a powerhouse global company that was going to use their services nationally and probably internationally.

This contract offered a tremendous financial benefit over the next one to three years, and Seth and Harold wanted this to be a factor in the valuation. The problem was their enthusiasm was based upon this new contract that currently produced no revenue. In essence Sam was saying, "But look what's coming. I want to get paid for that."

However, the buyer consistently asserted, "But look what's happened in the past. That's what I'm going to pay you for."

For Seth and Harold, we structured an earnout as follows. If revenue was received from this new global client, the buyer would pay the seller some percent of that for three years after closing. This was a win-win. The buyer did not pay for something that may not happen. That is, maybe the new customer would, in fact, not be a great customer. But if revenue did come in from this customer, the buyer was willing to pay a small portion of that to the seller. The seller was satisfied because they shared in the potential upside from this new client.

EARNOUTS SOLVE HOCKEY STICK PROJECTIONS

Frequently, sellers will show flat or slightly increasing revenue or profits for the past several years and predict tremendous growth in the coming years. Maybe the company has had one year of materially increased revenue or profit and now predicts that this will continue.

Here is a chart that will give you a visual of what I'm saying:

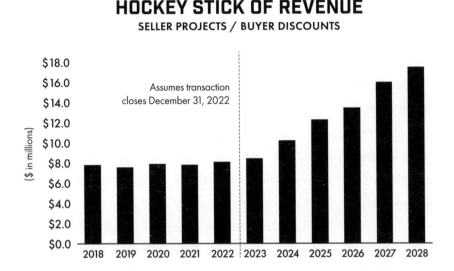

HOCKEY STICK OF REVENUE
SELLER PROJECTS / BUYER DISCOUNTS

Assumes transaction closes December 31, 2022

($ in millions)

Looking at this kind of uptick, the seller believes their company is worth more. The seller may believe that the revenue hockey stick is justified due to new contracts, increasing margins, or new lines of business.

However, buyers have a different perspective. They see hockey stick growth projections as unrealistic and not impacting value. The buyer could say, "I will pay more if that happens but shouldn't have to pay if it does not."

An earnout is the bridge. The risk of hockey stick growth is on the seller who is the party predicting the future. If the seller is right, then an earnout increases the purchase price. If the seller is wrong, the buyer hasn't "overpaid." Very often, the seller will stay involved in the business after closing in the short term to ensure that these growth projections occur.

In the above chart, revenue for 2022 is $8.1 million and has been reasonably flat for six years. Now the seller projects that revenue will more than double over the next five years. That is a pretty dramatic hockey stick.

A buyer will discount this, focusing on the current $8.5 million in revenue. In fact, without substantial evidence about why this growth story is true, some buyers would simply walk away, asserting lack of the seller's financial credibility.

Properly structured, an earnout is a way of sharing the risk.

This is a perfect situation for an earnout. If the seller is correct and this happens, the buyer and the seller will be happy, and it is fair for the buyer to pay more. However, if it does not happen, the buyer has not overpaid the seller.

Properly structured, an earnout is a way of sharing the risk. If the seeds planted by the seller bear more fruit, then the buyer is happy and can pay the seller more money. But if the seeds don't sprout, the buyer hasn't overpaid.

Unfortunately, earnouts have a bad reputation because they have been poorly structured, leading to disputes between the parties. Many earnouts have been based upon the future profitability of the company, which is a disaster waiting to happen.

Successful earnouts are not based upon profitability.

As a business person, you understand that profit is revenue minus expenses. However, after the transaction, the buyer has virtually 100 percent control over what those expenses are. For instance, if the buyer materially increases expenses after close, the projected profit will not be achieved, and the seller is going to be very disappointed.

A BETTER STRUCTURE FOR EARNOUTS

Successful earnouts are not based upon profitability. Earnouts should be structured on events that are clearly objective and binary. Revenue is binary. Signing a new client is binary. With binary terms, there is no room for dispute and no room for manipulation.[11]

But what happens if a company comes close but doesn't hit its revenue mark? For instance, assume the earnout required hitting $15 million in revenue within twelve months of closing. What if, at the end of twelve months, the revenue is $14.5 million or $14.9 million? The answer depends upon how the earnout is structured. Most earnouts will not pay out unless the company has achieved 90 percent or more of the target, with the "target" being the negotiated point.

Earnouts, properly structured, can work for both the seller and the buyer.

There are four ways sellers get paid: (1) cash at close, (2) seller financing, (3) equity rollover, and (4) earnout. Parties use these methods as tools to reach agreement on value and structure in order to close an acquisition. To achieve the win-win scenario, both sides need to understand these tools and have empathy and patience for the other party.

---

11   This is not 100 percent true. If the company has had 10 percent margins, the buyer has an interest in ensuring that revenue coming in has the same margins. The concern for the buyer is that the seller will jack up revenue to obtain their earnout, but that revenue will not be profitable for the buyer. There are two mechanisms that can come into play. One is that the seller cannot bring in any revenue that the buyer has not already approved. In this mechanism, the buyer gets to determine whether they want that revenue. If it's not profitable revenue, the buyer can say no. The other mechanism is that rather than creating an earnout based upon profitability, it could be based on gross profit that both the buyer and the seller agree on and the direct expenses associated with that profit. There is much less leeway for the buyer to manipulate expenses for a gross profit than for a net profit.

HOW DO SELLERS GET PAID?

CASH AT CLOSE	• Total cash received by Seller at Closing; net of escrow(s) Not contingent upon future operations • Typically, subject to capital gains tax rate	**50-80%** 100% = No Restructuring

+   **+**

SELLER NOTE/ FINANCING	• Seller provides debt financing to buyer (@capital gains) Seller note is subordinated to Buyer's other financing • Not contingent upon future operations	**10-20%**

+   **+**

ROLLOVER/ RETAINED EQUITY	• Seller retains an agreed-upon equity stake in company • Provides shared growth incentives for Seller and Buyer • Enables secondary liquidity event for Seller at new valuation	**10-25%**

+   **+**

EARNOUT (e.g. Revenue Share)	• Seller financial incentive contingent on future performance • Based on achieved performance against revenue targets • Bridges differences in valuation between seller and buyer	**10-30%**

LIFT OFF LESSONS

- There are four ways sellers get paid. It can be any combination of the following:
    1. Cash at close
    2. Seller financing
    3. Equity rollover
    4. Earnouts
- Potential buyers will be dubious if they are given what M&A professionals call "hockey stick stories." These are unrealistic projections about potential upsides, which may or may not happen, and should be avoided.
- Sellers are focused on the future and want to get paid for that. Buyers value the company based upon the company's past performance.
- Demonstrating significant growth in revenues, EBITDA, and EBITDA margins, along with upticks in sales—if supported by solid data—will interest buyers.
- Equity rollovers can be a way of getting a "second bite at the apple." It can be financially rewarding as well as a way of indicating to buyers that the seller believes in the future of the company.
- An earnout is a way of bridging the valuation gap, where the seller is focused on things that *will* happen, and the buyer only wants to pay for those things that *have* happened.
- Earnouts must be structured sensibly to avoid disputes between the parties.

CHAPTER 6

HOW DOES MY COMPANY GET VALUED?

So how does the market determine your company's value? There are so many textbooks on how to value companies, and these tomes fill libraries. This section will give you a very high-level understanding of how valuations work so that you have familiarity with the concepts and process.

Prior to even beginning a valuation, it is important to understand that most business sales are done on a "debt-free/cash-free" basis. This means that, subject to negotiation between the parties, the seller has to transfer a company with no debt—other than short-term payables—but gets to keep all cash in the company at close. If the seller has a line of credit or equipment loan or has factored receivables, these debts must be paid off at close (usually with purchase price proceeds). If the company has money in the bank, this belongs to the seller and is not considered part of the valuation of the company.

There are two primary methods of valuing privately held companies: (1) EBITDA multiple and (2) discounted cash flow. The EBITDA multiple is the prevalent valuation methodology in selling businesses, so we will focus on that. EBITDA is the company's net income <u>E</u>arnings <u>B</u>efore <u>I</u>nterest, <u>T</u>axes, <u>D</u>epreciation, and <u>A</u>mortization.

EBITDA MULTIPLE

I had a conversation with a potential seller recently about bringing his company to market. What the seller wanted to know—and what every seller wants to know—was the value of his company. After a thirty-minute discussion, I said that a real valuation would require a lot more work, but I gave a price range estimate.

> **The EBITDA multiple is the prevalent valuation methodology in selling businesses.**

He responded with "Well, when you look at my company, you're only looking at the numbers, but we are so much more than that! We have great relations with our customers, we have long-term customers, we have loyal employees. Don't we get more value for those and other things?"

I replied, "I understand what you are saying. However, all these other details have already been incorporated into the valuation range that I just gave you."

Understanding the EBITDA multiple valuation will make this clear.[12] The EBITDA multiple is where 80–90 percent of the conversation occurs regarding a company's valuation.

The EBITDA multiple valuation determines the company's value by multiplying a factor by the annual adjusted EBITDA. Let's assume the company has an adjusted EBITDA of $3 million a year. If the appropriate "factor" is 4, the company has a value of $12 million. But if the appropriate "factor" is 8, that same $3 million in EBITDA leads to a valuation of $24 million.

Clearly, determining the appropriate factor, or multiple, has a huge impact on the final value of the company. And the EBITDA multiple valuation methodology is one part science and one part art.

The science part is determining the company's adjusted EBITDA.

So what does that mean? EBITDA is a measure of the cash that a company generates or how much profit that machine produces. The net income on your profit and loss statement might include expenses that a new owner would not have to incur.[13] For instance, you have borrowed money from a bank and pay interest on those funds. A new buyer may not have to borrow money, so the interest that you paid gets added to your net income to reach EBITDA.

Here is an example.

I had a client who had $4 million in net income, after paying $200,000 a year in interest on $5 million of recently purchased equipment. To determine EBITDA, we added the $200,000 to the net income to reach EBITDA of $4.2 million.

You also want to be clear on the meaning of *depreciation* or *amortization*. These are accounting concepts that can reduce earnings for

---

12   The EBITDA multiple is a financial ratio that compares a company's enterprise value with its annual EBITDA.

13   A profit and loss statement details a business's income and expenses over a defined period.

tax purposes to reflect the declining value of an asset. For instance, the owner of the abovementioned company purchased $5 million in equipment that had a useful life of ten years. The owner could write off $500,000 a year in depreciation costs, which reduced taxes. But there was not a true cash outlay of $500,000 each year, so for purposes of determining EBITDA—how much cash the company was generating—this $500,000 was added back to the net income. The $4 million net income was increased by $200,000 (interest) and $500,000 (depreciation) to reach an EBITDA of $4.7 million.[14]

Of course, determining EBITDA is not always this clear. For instance, while taxes get added back to net income to determine EBITDA, not *all* taxes get added back. Income taxes are added back, but sales taxes, taxes paid on salaries to employees, and property taxes are not. You will need to work with an advisor to convert net income to EBITDA.

But EBITDA is not the final step! We also need to calculate adjusted EBITDA.[15]

Many owners run expenses through the company that are not truly necessary for the operations of the business. While I'm not the IRS, I have seen almost everything: kids who get allowances paid by the company, one or more cars (we had one company that had seven cars paid for by the company), vacations, renovations (sometimes to an office; occasionally to the owner's home), no-show employees (often parents or children), and much more. Sometimes owners prepay expenses or just run as many expenses as possible through the company to reduce taxable income. These expenses can be added

---

14 Amortization is the same as depreciation except that it applies to intangible assets. The concept and process are the same for amortization as depreciation.

15 Adjusted EBITDA is used throughout this book but also called normalized EBITDA.

to EBITDA to determine adjusted EBITDA, and these adjustments can add up.

Typical EBITDA adjustments are one-time expenses that are not going to be repeated or expenses that a buyer would not need to incur. For example, if you're paying your mother through the company, a buyer isn't going to do that. If you're paying her $50,000, I will reverse out that expense, which will leave an additional $50,000 available to the buyer.

We had one client with income statements showing negative net income, meaning the company was losing money. When we converted net income to EBITDA, the company became slightly profitable. When we made appropriate adjustments, including removing personal expenses that were run through the company, the adjusted EBITDA was over $1 million.

We have also worked with companies where there were no EBITDA adjustments. EBITDA adjustments are unique to every company and are very fact-specific. The seller will need to show any adjustments to the potential buyer and be able to justify why the buyer will not need those expenses. For instance, personal cars that are run through the business can be subject to an EBITDA adjustment. However, cars or trucks that are used in the business cannot be adjusted out.

Occasionally, sellers want to reverse expenses that cannot be reversed. I had a seller tell me, "I won't be at the company, so you can take out my $250,000 salary."

To which I responded, "No, you're not going to be at the company, but somebody's going to take your role, and they're going to need to get paid. I can't reverse that out."

In contrast, if the seller has a salary of $500,000 and the market-based salary for their position is $200,000, then $300,000 in salary can be reversed.

Adding in and taking out legitimate expenses is called "normalization." Let's assume that your company is going to be 5 times multiple. If we're able to adjust your normalizations for $100,000 at 5 times, that means an extra $500,000 in value to the company. If the company was 10 times multiple and it had a million dollars in adjustments, that means an extra $10,000,000 in value to the company. EBITDA normalizations can really add up.

By the way, the normalization process can sometimes result in a *reduction* of EBITDA. There have been times where we have had to decrease the EBITDA because the company isn't spending what it should on things such as finance, or business development, or the owner took a substantially below-market salary. For instance, we had one owner who was running their company on a $75,000 salary. Hiring someone to do the job the owner was performing would require $200,000/year. In this situation, the buyer will need to spend more than what the seller was spending, and EBITDA is adjusted down.

These are some of the factors that determine how adjusted EBITDA is reached.

However, this is only half of the process. Now we come to the art part—determining the applicable multiple.

THE APPLICABLE MULTIPLE

If a company has $3 million of adjusted EBITDA and the appropriate multiple is 10, that means the company is valued at $30 million. If the multiple is 3, that is a $9 million company. Same $3 million in adjusted EBITDA, but the value of the company could be dramatically different based upon the multiple. While the adjusted EBITDA has not changed, the multiple used dramatically changes the value of the company.

Determining the appropriate multiple starts with the industry. There are norms, usually a range, for most industries. For instance, construction firms may have multiples between 3 and 7, while manufacturing companies might have a multiple range of 5 to 9. A SaaS (software as a service) company is likely to have a multiple range of 15 or more.[16] Therefore, we start with the industry norms.

There are many factors that impact the appropriate multiple for a company. Here are the most common ones:

- Margins
  - □ Are the margins for your company above or below the margins for companies in your industry?

- Company Size
  - □ A basic reality (maybe unfairness) of the world is that smaller companies get lower multiples. Smaller companies are often subject to more volatility, such as the loss of a single customer can have a devastating impact on revenue. That is less likely in a larger company. Let's assume that companies A and B are in the same industry, serving the same kinds of customers, and even have similar margins. However, company A has $3 million in adjusted EBITDA, and company B has $10 million in adjusted EBITDA, so company B will get a higher multiple than company A.

---

16 In some industries, valuation is determined as a multiple of revenue, not adjusted EBITDA. This is rare and usually applies to fast-growing, software-based companies.

- Revenue
  - Has revenue been increasing, remaining consistent, or declining for the last five years? I worked with one company that had five years of declining revenues. It's still a pretty attractive company with $30 million in revenue and decent margins, but five years of declining revenue lowered the multiple.

- Customer Concentration
  - Does the company have more than 20 percent of its revenue coming from a specific customer? Do the largest three customers represent more than 50 percent of the revenue of a firm? Higher customer concentration means higher risk, which can mean a lower multiple.

- Recurring Revenue
  - Does the company need to find new customers each year, or does it have a stable and recurring customer base? For instance, assume that a company is in the residential roofing business that has an EBITDA multiple range of 3 to 8. If the company must find new homes to work on each year, it will have a lower multiple than if it worked for insurance companies that insure and pay for repairs of homeowners' roofs.

- Strength of Management Team
  - If the owners of the company are the primary management, the company will be less valuable than if there is a strong management team outside ownership. As discussed in previous chapters, here is the test I ask potential sellers: if the owners were to get hit by lightning tomorrow, would the company continue to function as

it did yesterday? If not, the company will have a lower multiple. The lack of a strong management team outside ownership might make the company unsellable.

- Stability of Employees
  - Does the company have long-term employees who perform well, or is there a lot of staff turnover?

- Vendor Concentration
  - Is there a critical component used in the business that can only be supplied from a single vendor? Even if there are multiple vendors, does the company get significantly preferred pricing? Is that pricing ensured through a long-term contract, or is it based on the relationship between the owner and the vendor?

- Strengths of Processes in the Company
  - For example, are the financial records well maintained? Is there a functioning electronic record management system? How are new employees?

For practical purposes, let's compare two companies.

Example: HVAC company serving residential customers with the following characteristics:[17]

---

17   The charts included give a general overview, but a more detailed look is needed when you are selling your company. Consult your M&A advisor for more information.

RESIDENTIAL HVAC COMPANY NO. 1				
Year	Revenue	Margin	Adjusted EBITDA	% of Recurring Revenue
2022	$22M	15%	$3.3M	40%
2021	$20M	15%	$3M	35%
2020	$18M	15%	$2.7M	30%
2019	$16M	15%	$2.4M	20%
2018	$14M	15%	$2.1M	15%

As you may have noticed, over the last several years, virtually every residential HVAC company offers a "services maintenance contract" for a flat fee with a reduction on repairs when necessary. These services contracts offer "recurring" revenue and create a stickier relationship with the customer. An HVAC company that gets 40 percent of its revenue from these service contract customers will be more valuable than an HVAC company that is solely project based.

Further, let's say that for the residential HVAC industry, the multiple range is 3 to 10 for companies up to $100 million in revenue, 12 percent margins, revenue growth of 10 percent, and recurring revenue of 20 percent.

The strengths of this company are increasing revenue, above-market margins, and significantly above-market recurring revenue. The challenges are that the company has below-market revenue growth (which, as a percentage, is actually slowing each year) and is on the smaller size of the industry. While there is a lot more to know (level of customer concentration, importance of ownership to the management of the company, stability of employees, strength of processes, etc.), this company is likely to get a 5–8 multiple. However, only deep analysis of all the other factors will allow a judgment to be reached as to whether the multiple should be 5 or 8.

Compare the aforementioned company with the following:

RESIDENTIAL HVAC COMPANY NO. 2				
Year	Revenue	Margin	Adjusted EBITDA	% of Recurring Revenue
2022	$75M	10%	$7.5M	20%
2021	$72M	9%	$7.2M	20%
2020	$70M	7%	$7M	10%
2019	$85M	16%	$8.5M	0%
2018	$80M	14%	$8M	0%

This company is very different, and the data tells a story. First, the company is much larger, and such companies get higher multiples. But what happened between 2019 and 2020? Both revenue and margins declined—a lot. However, for the first time, the company had some recurring revenue that substantially increased over the next few years. My supposition would be that the owner wanted to sell, knowing that revenue was high and margins were great, but was disappointed that the multiple wasn't high because of the lack of recurring revenue. The owner then restructured the company to temporarily sacrifice revenue and margin to build the recurring revenue base. Recurring revenue at a lower margin may, in fact, be worth more than higher margin work that is not recurring. This company is likely to get a 7–10 multiple, although, again, there is a lot of work that would need to be done to reach a reasonable conclusion.

Here's something to keep in mind: Your company's valuation should be a range, not a specific number. There are too many factors and too much judgment involved to reach a precise number. You need to be open to market data.

MARKET REALITIES

I noted earlier that you need to have a hardheaded mindset, and here's why: your company is worth what a buyer is willing to spend. If potential buyers with the realistic ability to buy your company value your company differently than what an adjusted EBITDA multiple valuation shows, that gives you the real market value.

When you go to market, humility is always required. We worked with one company that, based upon careful analysis, we valued at $50–$60 million. We went to market without putting a price on the company but gave potential buyers the relevant data then asked buyers to submit a proposed purchase price. The company sold for over $70 million because the buyer (unknown to us at the time) was in the process of acquiring another company that would be far more valuable if combined with my client's company. There is no way we could have known that when we went to market, but we were all delighted with the result.

Your company is worth what a buyer is willing to spend.

In contrast, we worked with one company that we estimated to have a market value of between $17 and $20 million. After speaking with many potential buyers, the offers all were between $14 and $15 million. While there was customer concentration, we argued that it should not be a significant concern because of concentration in the industry. Every potential buyer disagreed with us, and we were surprised by the consistency of the offers. The market had spoken. Ultimately, the seller sold at the market value of $15 million.

SELLER AMBITIONS VERSUS MARKET REALITIES

Frequently, a business owner will tell me they want to sell their company for a specific amount, say $15 million, or that their company should have an 8 times EBITDA multiple.[18] I often chuckle at this because when I ask how the owner arrived at these numbers, I'm told, "I was talking to my buddy during a round of golf, and he told me what his company is worth. Well, mine is worth more than his!" In other words, the owner has no idea what an EBITDA multiple is or how it's arrived at.

When I explore with the business owner how they reached that conclusion, the answer usually falls into one of the following categories:

- A financial advisor has reviewed the financial goals of the owner and concluded that the owner needs a specific amount to retire.
- The owner has talked with friends or colleagues who sold their businesses and estimated the value of their company based upon those discussions.
- The purchase price is a report card for the owner (i.e., the owner has put so much time, energy, and sweat equity into the company that the owner feels that it ought to be worth that price).
- The owner feels their company is special (strong ties with customers, great long-term employees, fills a specific niche in the market, etc.) that normal financial metrics should not apply.

---

18   Multiple is the factor applied to your adjusted EBITDA to arrive at a valuation of your business.

These considerations are interesting and essentially determine the *ambition* of the owner. However, none of these considerations are based upon a deep understanding of the market value of the specific business. In fact, most of these factors are completely irrelevant to determining the value of your company because of the following:

- The amount of money needed to achieve your financial goals is important but could be significantly more or less than what your company is worth. There is no correlation between what you need and the value of your company.
- Discussions with friends (often golfing buddies, I have learned) and colleagues are likely to be slightly more useful if the comparison is to similarly situated companies. However, two companies in the same industry could provide very different clients, offer different products or services, have different margins, etc. This is a place to start, not end.
- The personal report card or feeling that your company is special is an emotional response. It is good to know, important to respect, but irrelevant to determining the value of your company.

Always remember that you are the decision maker of what to do with your company. If you don't like the market value, you can continue to own and run your company. No one can force you to sell. However, if you want to retire, have a health issue, or some other factor is drawing you to a sale, you may have some hard, personal decisions to confront.

For example, we were hired by a family-owned company that had profits of $2 million per year. This family was extremely good at building and managing their business, and they decided that their company was worth at least $40 to $45 million. After doing our market research, I had to go to them and say, "You have a fantastic company. You really do. But realistically, the market is going to value this as a $20 million company, and we can get to that $20 million from lots of different ways. If you would like to continue to own your company indefinitely, I understand. As the owner, you get to decide what you want to do. But for your company to be a $40 million company, you're going to need closer to $5 million in profits."

As the conversation continued, my team and I realized that we did not feel we could help these owners because their expectations were not consistent with what we thought the market was going to be. We parted ways on good terms. Several years later, we touched base again. The company still had not sold.

RISKS ASSUMED BY NOT BEING REALISTIC

Throughout this chapter, I've stressed the importance of being realistic about your company. Here is a no-holds-barred truth about why this is so important.

Let's say that your company's market range of values should be between $16 and $20 million, but you are not willing to be realistic. You think it's worth $30 million, and you're not going to sell it for less than that. There is always the *possibility* that somebody will offer you that $30 million, even though the company, by normal metrics, is only worth at the most $20 million. Are you willing to take that risk? Are you willing to let your company sit on the market with potential buyers passing you by because you're waiting for the "big" offer?

Remember this mantra: time kills deals.

Markets change on a whim, and every day brings different factors, some good and some bad. By holding out for that above-market price, bad things could happen.

Here are two examples:

- In November 2019 we sold a company for over $50 million. In March 2020 the global COVID-19 pandemic temporarily closed the economy, causing revenues to decline 90 percent. Had my client still owned the company, the value upon sale after the pandemic would have been materially less, at least for several years. The company itself had not changed, but factors way outside of the owner's control had changed. If the owners had not sold in November 2019, waiting just a few more months to see if they could get a better price, they might still own their company or have sold for materially less.

- Bob and Alan owned a $14 million revenue company that distributed rugged electronic equipment for a global equipment manufacturer. Their business was growing, and Bob and Alan were ready to sell. We found a terrific buyer, and the transaction closed. Two weeks after closing, the global equipment manufacturer announced—due to supply chain challenges also related to the pandemic—no equipment would be shipped to distributors for at least six months. Once again, Bob and Alan did nothing wrong, but their company would've been worth a lot less two weeks after the deal than when the deal actually closed.

Always remember, by holding out for an out-of-market valuation, you are taking on a lot of risk. You'll need to either have a lot of patience while waiting for your "ideal deal" or adjust your expectations back to what the market is telling you. Either way, it's your choice because you're always in control.

LIFT OFF LESSONS

- Ambition does not determine the value of your company; the market does.
- Be fair and honest when determining what expenses to report and which ones to leave out; your EBITDA number will be scrutinized by buyers.
- EBITDA stands for net income Earnings Before Interest, Taxes, Depreciation, and Amortization.
- Fair or not, the reality is that smaller companies get lower "multiples," which is the number that EBITDA gets multiplied by.
- There are many factors that go into a buyer's assessment of a "multiple," including the following:
  - Margins
  - Company Size
  - Revenue
  - Customer Concentration
  - Recurring Revenue
  - Strength of Management Team
  - Strength of Employees
  - Vendor Concentration
  - Policies and Procedures

CHAPTER 7

WHO WILL BUY MY COMPANY?

As the founder/owner of your company, you may have a plethora of ideas about who might buy your company, and there may be several prospective suitors. However, there is a difference between who might buy your company and who will buy your company. Here's an example from another client of mine.

Brian and Sally, a married couple who raised two children and built a $50 million company together, want to sell their company to travel the world. They have an experienced management team but no one who is capable or interested in acquiring the company.

Brian says his desired buyer is someone who understands their business, has experience with their client base, and has previously operated a company with at least fifty employees.

Sally tells me that she highly values "certainty of close."

Brian then says that under no circumstance will they sell to a financial firm.

There is one final restriction: no information about their company can be shared with an actual or potential competitor prior to close.

This is a problem.

In most situations, you cannot find an operating company buyer who is not an actual or potential competitor. In this instance, financial firms, such as PE, are off the table. There are no employees interested in a management buyer. And searchers raise many concerns about the certainty of close.

In most transactions, everyone needs to be a little flexible. And in this one, we were ultimately able to structure a deal that met most, but not all, of Brian and Sally's criteria.

I hear these kinds of requirements about buyers frequently.

Sellers who understand more about the universe of buyers have an easier time than those that make hard-and-fast rules. Buyers come in many shapes and flavors, with positives and negatives associated with each.

As in most of life, we live with trade-offs. This chapter discusses the strengths and weaknesses of each type of buyer, many of whom will fit in more than one category.

The basic categories of buyers are the following:

- Strategic
- Private Equity
- Management Buyout
- Generational Transfers
- Searchers

STRATEGIC ACQUIRERS

Most owners tell me that they want to sell to "a strategic," by which they mean a company that operates in their industry. Business owners often like the idea of a competitor wanting to buy their company.

I know sellers who feel like a "strategic sale" is "winning" because the buyer/competitor believes that it is better to pay money for the target than continue to compete against that target or build what the target delivers themselves.

There is also the hope that because the buyer already knows the target industry, the company's continued success is likely. And in fact, the seller may already know the buyer, having met at conferences or industry events over the years. And sometimes strategics will pay more than other potential buyers because there can be synergies that add value and can be shared between the buyer and the seller.

It makes sense, but there are problems.

To close an acquisition, the buyer—or any buyer—will need to learn a lot of confidential information about your company. A buyer that operates in your industry is likely to be a competitor or at least a potential competitor.

As a seller, you must be prepared to share information with an actual or potential competitor in order to sell your company to a strategic.

The general benefits of selling to a strategic buyer are the following:

- You as the seller may already know the buyer, which might give you comfort. And if it does not give you comfort, you should not do the transaction.
- The buyer has experience in your industry, so the transition time is likely to be less than with other buyers.

- The buyer already knows the strengths and challenges of the industry, so due diligence is likely to be more targeted and possibly less time-consuming.
- Strategic buyers often offer the highest purchase price because the synergies between the buyer and the seller can create more value, which the buyer can share with the seller. Understand that these synergies are not issues such as reducing back-office duplication but in the realm of opening new markets or offering new products or services to existing customers.

Of course, there are also drawbacks to strategic buyers.

- A strategic buyer is usually a current or potential competitor. As a seller, you will have to share a lot of information about your company with the buyer without the certainty that the transaction will close. If the deal does not close, and not all transactions do, the potential buyer knows about your secret sauce—your most important employees, relationships, processes, margins, marketing strategy, and all matters hidden behind the curtain. Every potential buyer will sign an NDA, but the seller cannot remove the information that the buyer now holds in their memory if the transaction does not close.
- Sellers often value their corporate culture. A strategic buyer will have its own culture. There may be similarities with the seller, but there will be differences as well. Upon the acquisition, the culture of the seller generally gives way to the culture of the buyer. It may not be immediate but usually happens over a two- to three-year period.
- Most strategic buyers have deep experience in operating companies but not necessarily in buying companies. They may not have standards for how to proceed with an acquisi-

tion and may be feeling their way through the M&A process. A seller should ask how many transactions the strategic buyer has done in the last year or two to determine whether the buyer has experience with M&A. If they do not, they should have advisors who are sophisticated and experienced at getting transactions closed.

- Strategic buyers can be subject to internal politics that might impact or even kill the acquisition. The seller needs to understand the underlying dynamics of the strategic buyer to understand the risk to close.

- Even if there is not a change of personnel at the buyer, there can be a change in strategic direction, which can have an effect. If the buyer changes direction, the transaction may no longer be of interest.

- A strategic buyer is usually a corporate entity and may not have universal agreement on the chosen strategy. For instance, the strategic buyer might be interested in pursuing a new sector or an expansion into a new area of business that is the motivation for the acquisition. Employees of the buyer might disagree, create dissention, and throw sand in the gears of the acquisition.

PRIVATE EQUITY

There was a time when private equity (PE) firms were looked upon as the pirates of the business world. Even today some sellers think of PE as evil, cold-blooded capitalists interested in cutting expenses by firing employees, unconcerned with morale or even the quality of the products or services of the company.

In this construct, the only goal of PE is to raise revenue, reduce expenses, and sell the company again before the house of cards collapses.

I've had owners tell me, "I'll never sell to a PE! They're like the vultures circling the sky. And they're looking for either dying companies or healthy companies where they can squeeze out all the juice."

The world is more complicated than this image.

Of course, there are some PE that are focused only on the numbers. But there has been a sea change in the PE industry over the last two decades.

PE used to focus only on acquisitions of companies that had hundreds of millions, or billions, of revenues. In the last several decades, a significant portion of PE buyers have become very interested in companies that are far smaller and that are still owned by the founder/owner.

Studies have shown that companies that reach a certain level of success with the founder/owner can create strong platforms for future growth. PE interested in this part of the market respects the founder/owner and the culture of the firm that has been created. With acquisition they also have a primary interest in promoting growth.

While the founder/owner can create and grow strong, healthy companies, the owner tends not to have experience in "optimizing" the company. PE knows that there are value enhancements that can be unlocked without changing the culture of the company. For instance, PE can facilitate growth by adding capital to accelerate growth. PE may also have extensive back-office experience to increase efficiency without impacting quality.

I have found that many PE firms have great respect for the owner/founder. The respectful PE says, "This owner has taken an idea and grown a multimillion-dollar company. Sure, this owner doesn't have an MBA, but he has built a business from their kitchen table that now has $20, $40, $60 million of revenue. That is a big deal! I, Mr. PE, didn't do that. But I know how to take that company and turn it from a $60 million company to a $300 million company. That's the type of partnership I want to create between the founder/owner and me, the PE firm."

There are as many flavors of PE as there are flavors of ice cream.

There is PE that has funds under management, PE that raises equity for each transaction, PE that looks for sellers willing to stay with the company long term and others who expect only a three-month transition. Some PE plan to sell companies after five to seven years, and others want to hold companies for decades. Some PE might be interested in only buying control of the company; some PE focus on minority investments.

To know if PE can be the right buyer for your company, you need to learn about specific PE buyers. But first, ask if the goal of the PE firm is consistent with your goals. If not, walk away. If so, explore further. Here are some factors to consider when working with PE:

- PE are professional buyers of companies. Acquisitions by PE tend to move quickly because the buyer and advisors are experienced.

- Most PE firms have access to capital to close transactions, increasing the certainty of close. However, you want to know whether the PE has funds under management or whether they raise capital for each deal. While raising capital for each transaction may seem riskier, the seller needs to know whether the PE has successfully raised capital on a deal-by-deal basis before. It's important for the seller to understand the level of risk for the PE getting the debt and equity to close a transaction.

- PE is more likely to respect and maintain the culture of the acquired company unless the plan is to merge the acquired company with another operating entity. You need to understand the PE plan for your company. Will your company be a "platform" investment, a stand-alone company, or is it part of a "roll up" strategy. The PE's plans will give you a sense of the likelihood of maintaining your firm's culture.

- What do you as the seller want to do after the transaction? Some PE are only interested in investing in the existing management team; other firms are interested in bringing in their own management.

- The PE firm might be an expert in your industry and, hence, likely to be actively involved in the ongoing operations of your company. Other PE invest "opportunistically," looking for strong companies without focusing on specific industries. Opportunistic PE will provide capital, oversight, and business advice without delving into the day-to-day operation of your company.

- Most PE will require the seller to "roll over" equity. For instance, the seller will own 10 to 25 percent of the company after the acquisition. As previously discussed, rollover equity offers the seller a second bite of the apple by sharing in the future growth of the company. When dealing with PE, a seller should learn early in the process whether the PE firm will require rollover equity and at what percentage, as well as the PE's plan for exiting the investment. Rollover equity could be profitable if the buyer wants to sell in three to five years but far less profitable if the buyer plans to hold the investment indefinitely. There also can be provisions for the buyer to purchase the seller's rollover equity in the event there is no second transaction.

The bottom line is do not paint PE, or any other potential buyer, with too broad a brush.

PE should be considered as a buyer, but the seller needs to know a lot about the specific PE firm to determine whether there is an alignment of interests between the parties.

MANAGEMENT BUYOUTS

A management buyout (MBO) occurs when one or more employees acquire the company from the owner. When I raise this possibility, most sellers immediately say, "None of my employees have the capital needed to acquire my company."

That is usually true but does not make MBOs impossible.

For example, Donna owned a consulting company and wanted to sell. Karen, the chief operating officer, was involved in identifying potential buyers and was preparing the materials needed to bring the company to market. Over a cup of coffee, I asked Karen if she had considered buying Donna's company. She had but had no idea how to accomplish this seemingly impossible task. With our assistance, Karen ended up purchasing Donna's company.

There are two questions to consider in an MBO.

The first question is, "Can the employees make the transition from being a salaried employee to accepting the risks of entrepreneurship?" To state the obvious, employees have certainty about their income level, which will be paid on a predictable schedule. This predictability has less risk when paying a mortgage, financing a child's education, planning vacations, and other expenses in life. In fact, it is easier to get a mortgage as an employee than as an entrepreneur. The transition to entrepreneur can be unsettling; if revenue declines because a major client cancels a contract, the entrepreneur is the first to take the hit.

There is a military phrase that applies to business: leaders eat last.

Good entrepreneurs will make sure that their employees get paid, even if that means they go without a salary. Even when the company is profitable, entrepreneurs may limit distributions to reinvest in the company.

The right MBO buyer is aware of the risk and willing to accept and manage it. The MBO buyer that will be terrified of this risk is the wrong buyer. Just because the MBO buyer/employee has been critical in running the company doesn't mean that person is going to make a good owner. There needs to be some serious thought by both the seller and the potential new owner as to whether the MBO team is the right mix of people.

Leaders eat last.

After you've determined that the highly competent employees can make the transition to the mentality of entrepreneur, the second question is, "How do you finance the acquisition?"

Most employees will not have millions to fund the acquisition. For smaller transactions, the employee may be able to get a loan guaranteed by the Small Business Administration (SBA) for up to $5 million. The buyer will need to bring at least 5 to 10 percent of the purchase price and transaction costs to the closing in equity. Sometimes buyers can take funds from retirement accounts or get investments from friends and family. For instance, if the buyer has no access to capital or if the transaction is too big to be financed with an SBA loan, the buyer can find investors (usually PE) willing to provide the equity to complete the transaction. Of course, the equity providers will own a significant piece of the company after closing, but the management team can own part of the company acquired without taking cash out of their pocket. In many cases, the MBO purchasers will be required to personally guarantee debt.

As previously noted, the seller can assist the management team by providing seller financing or accepting equity roll. Sellers are often more willing to provide this financial assistance for a management team that has worked at the company for years.

Here is an interesting twist. Many employees want to be the owner so they can be the boss. As most entrepreneurs know, however, if you have equity investors or lenders, the entrepreneur can rightly consider those parties the real boss. The MBO buyer may be the boss to the remaining employees, but banks and/or equity investors can be the boss to the owner.

Many employees want to be the owner so they can be the boss.

There is another benefit to selling in an MBO.

As I have noted before, on the day of closing, the seller will always know more about the company than the buyer will. That's not true in an MBO. This is one of the few circumstances where the person who is buying the company knows just about as much as the person who is selling the company. This is terrific because it means that due diligence is easier, and there is preexisting trust between the parties. The buyer is aware of the strengths and challenges facing the company and wants to move forward.

However, there is a potential downside to MBOs: very often, these transactions do not provide the same "cash at close" that a third-party buyer would offer the seller. As stated above, the seller may provide seller financing and equity rollover at higher levels than would be available to a third party.

GENERATIONAL TRANSFERS

Historically, companies were handed from parent to child. In the last forty years, this has become less common, as many children of business owners are not interested in owning the business. In some ways, generational transfers have the characteristics of an MBO with the added complexity of family dynamics. This generally makes a transaction more challenging.

There are books written on transferring your company to a child or grandchild. If this is your situation, please do a lot of reading and thinking. An intergenerational transfer can be a fantastic family legacy, but it can cause untold stress within the family. Here are some considerations:

- Does the buyer want the company as much as the current owner wants to pass on the company within the family?
- Is the seller willing to allow the next generation to run the company differently?
- Is the seller willing to accept minimal liquidity at close in order to allow a family member to acquire the company without substantial debt?

I have seen many situations where the next generation does not want the company but does not want to disappoint or fight with their family. The seller may be in their sixties or seventies, and the buyer is in their thirties or forties. There might well be a generationally based difference in comfort with technology. I have seen situations where the seller was opposed to new technology, saying, "We tried that, and it didn't work" or "What we are doing is successful. Why would you mess that up?" The seller needs to think about whether changes to the company will have negative generational impacts, not to mention Thanksgiving dinner.

SEARCHERS

Searchers are a new category of buyers. A searcher is usually an entrepreneur focused on acquiring, managing, and growing a single private company. Think of them as PE that is looking to operate the company and not seeking to own more than one company.

Searchers also come in all shapes and sizes. There are some who have the capital to fund a transaction or are already backed by a PE fund. In those situations, funding is reasonably secure. Conversely, there are others who must raise the capital for the specific transaction.

Seller beware: this can be a real risk and very time-consuming. Remember they are only seeking to acquire one company, so they do not have a track record for raising this capital. Like PE, searchers may plan on exiting the company after five to seven years or plan on an indefinite hold. All the factors that we discussed on PE apply to searchers. It's not that searchers are good or bad; they are all different, and you need to know whether there is an alignment of interests.

SUMMARY

As is usual, the world is more complicated than theory. While this chapter discusses the various categories of buyers, in the real world, there can be a merging of these categories. We closed one transaction that was led by a strategic acquirer who was backed by PE. Similarly, MBOs and family acquisitions can be funded by financial firms seeking to invest in companies but not run them.

Regardless of the category of buyer, it is important to avoid tire kickers. They will waste your time and put your confidential information at risk.

LIFT OFF LESSONS

- There are five basic categories of buyers: strategic, private equity, management buyout, generational transfers, and searchers.

- Strategics may know your industry and may even pay the highest purchase price, but the seller must know they are providing confidential information to an actual or potential competitor.

- There are many kinds of PE, so don't be so fast to exclude PE. Some will pay good value if they like a company and may hold it for a long time. PE deals also often offer—and sometimes require—a "second bite at the apple" for sellers.

- PE and searchers have been proven to grow companies successfully.

- MBOs and generational transfers provide less liquidity at close for the seller but are often the best way to preserve the legacy of the firm. However, these buyers must understand that leaders eat last; employees must be paid before new management gets paid.

- Bottom line: get to know your buyer, and assess if they're the right one for you.

CHAPTER 8

WHAT ARE THE STAGES OF THE PROCESS?

The sales process depends upon whether you are selling to an already identified buyer—as in the case of an MBO or an intergenerational transfer—or whether the transaction is likely to be an arm's-length transfer to a buyer who may not yet be known. This chapter focuses on the process for the latter situation, as this is much more common.

The process for selling your company in an arm's-length transaction has three distinct phases:

Phase 1: Preparation

Phase 2: Buyer Identification

Phase 3: LOI to Closing

During each of these phases, as the seller, you have one overriding responsibility: operating your company. It is extremely easy to get distracted by the sales process; it is exciting, nerve racking, and emotional, with lots of highs and lows. The temptation to focus on the sales process and not the day-to-day issues of your company is a major mistake made by sellers.

SELL SIDE REPRESENTATION

PREPARATION

PHASE 1
30-45 Days

- Compilation/Analysis of Financials and Client Concentration
- Assess Market Position: Review Strengths & Challenges
- Data Room Established
- CIM/Teaser Completed
- Legal Review of NDA
- Prepare List of Potential Buyers

BUYER IDENTIFICATION

PHASE 2
1-6 Months
after Phase I ends

- Market Outreach Begins
- NDAs Signed and Catalogued
- Respond to Inquiries from Potential Buyers
- Buyer Qualification
- Extensive Due Diligence
- Management Meetings
- Letter of Intent (LOI) Negotiations
- Ends when LOI is Signed

SELLER MUST CONTINUE TO FOCUS ON RUNNING THE COMPANY
e.g. Contract Delivery and Business Development

LOI TO CLOSE

PHASE 3
2-4 Months
after Phase II ends

- Extensive Confirmatory Due Diligence
- Financing Obtained
- Negotiation of Legal Documents (Legal and Commercial Terms)
- Ends when Closing Occurs

PHASE 1: PREPARATION

GATHERING MATERIALS AND
PERFORMING SELF DUE DILIGENCE

Phase 1 is focused on preparation, because no matter how prepared you think you are, I can tell you from experience that you are not fully prepared. Your advisors, and ultimately the buyers, will ask you for documents you can't find, questions you have never thought about, and projections about the future that are outside your control. You know a lot about your company, but outsiders will look at it in a totally different manner. My advice: Be humble. Be empathetic. Be patient.

The process will start by creating a *data room*, an electronic secure repository for all documents and analysis based on those documents. This will involve three to five years of financial statements (balance sheet and profit and loss), tax returns, customer breakdowns, number and identity of employees, salaries, work in progress, sales projections, and much more.

An electronic data room allows you to open information to a buyer in stages. There is a lot of information that a buyer does not need to know to decide whether or not to move forward. Think of the data room as a series of gates beginning with high-level information and getting more granular as the process continues.

A mistake that sellers frequently make is only gathering the data needed for each gate, leaving them scrambling to gather more information as the process continues. There will be so much happening throughout the process that you want to be prepared for those items that absolutely will be required to close a transaction, leaving you time to deal with the negotiations and unexpected requests. This preparation pays off. Buyers are judging how knowledgeable you are about your company and how organized the company is. If you can respond to a buyer request with "Yes, we have that prepared and can open that material for you today," then the buyer's confidence increases. Conversely, if the seller is unable to respond to data requests for days or even weeks, a buyer becomes more concerned about the maturity of the company.

After the information is gathered, you have to evaluate this information from the perspective of a potential buyer by conducting due diligence on your own company. This is harder than it seems.

You understand why your chart of accounts is set up in a specific manner, why you accrue for certain expenses on a quarterly (or annual) basis as opposed to monthly, and a myriad of other issues. You *know* your company. In fact, you are so familiar with running your company there are details that you take for granted or possibly overlook. But the buyer does not know what you know. The buyer is an outsider expressly focused on judging your company and its value.

The buyer is an outsider expressly focused on judging your company and its value.

Be prepared for the buyer's questions. Are the financials compiled, reviewed, or audited? Have there been any tax issues? What analysis of state and local tax issues has been done? Is there is a union? Any litigation, even if resolved? Any regulatory concerns? Churn in the staff? Customer concentration? What will the buyer see when they look at your company?

A friend was getting ready to sell his beautifully renovated house. While visiting, I noticed that the bathroom faucet was leaking, there was a water stain in the ceiling, and there were cracks in the kitchen tiles. When I pointed these out to my friend, he looked shocked; those problems had been there so long that he had stopped noticing them.

I said those will be the first items that a potential buyer sees, not the double atrium entranceway or the lovely master bedroom suite.

During the sales process, your company will be exposed to buyers (and their advisors) looking for problems that you have overlooked. Sellers need to know what a buyer is going to see and correct anything that can be corrected or have explanations for the "problems." The very act of compiling materials may reveal patterns or challenges that were not otherwise obvious.

For instance, a client had a company with an extremely high net working capital, and the company needed to keep a lot of cash on its balance sheet. When we gathered and reviewed the financials, I said to my client, "You're getting paid by your clients in sixty to ninety days, but you're paying your vendor in thirty days. You're not only running a company. You're also running a bank. You're basically lending money to your vendors from your accounts receivable that hasn't been turned into cash yet. A buyer isn't going to like that."

My client replied, "Sharon, you don't understand. Our customers are Fortune 1000 companies. We know we're going to get paid. It might take up to ninety days, but we will get paid. In contrast, our vendors are small operators, two- and three-man shops, that do mechanical or electronic work for us, and they need to get their money quickly. By ensuring they get paid in thirty days, they will drop any other jobs to work for us. Yes, we know that it costs us something to pay our vendors early and to carry our accounts receivable from our clients. But it gives us a very significant strategic advantage. Those vendors are critically important to our business."

"I completely understand," I said. "Thank you for clarifying. Now I understand that something a buyer would see as a problem is actually a strength."

When we brought this company to market, we would immediately tell potential buyers, "Please notice that the company is paid by clients in ninety days but pays vendors in thirty days. That is a strength because they have a loyal vendor base that gives them flexibility to take on more work." As a result, this "problem" never became an issue with potential buyers, who now saw this as a company strength.

Every company presents its own challenges.

I had a client who owned a manufacturing company. Upon gathering the data, we saw that 89 percent of their customers were actually tied to a single Fortune 500 company. This would usually be an unacceptable level of client concentration, resulting in a price reduction. Upon closer inspection, it was clear this Fortune 500 company actually had multiple offices that decided independently who to hire. My client had relationships with seventeen different offices, and each of those offices made separate buying decisions. We, of course, disclosed both the client concentration and the reason we did not consider this a problem. The final buyer agreed with our analysis, and this challenging issue faded away.

This self due diligence is also the time for you to consider the appropriate value or the valuation of your company. It is important to remember that your company is ultimately worth what a capable buyer is willing to spend. As the seller, you are not required to sell if you don't like the market value, but you should begin the process with some sense of how a third party is likely to value your company.

PREPARING MARKETING MATERIALS

Phase 1 is when the marketing materials are prepared. There are two core documents: a teaser and a confidential information memorandum (CIM).

A teaser is a one- or two-page document that gives a high-level overview of the selling company. It would include the products or services offered, markets served, and financial data (revenue and profit). It does not include the name of the selling company and should be drafted so that readers of the teaser are not able to determine the identity of the seller. The purpose of the teaser is to find buyers who are interested in learning more.

At the end of this book, there is a dynamic QR code. That QR code will lead you to a model teaser.

The CIM—sometimes referred to as "the book"—provides information about the company for sale and the reasons the company is being transferred. I have seen CIMs that are one-hundred-plus pages of dense text with details about the company's financials, customers, projected growth, employees, and many charts. While this used to be the norm, over the last fifteen years, there have been two major changes. First, just like the data room has "gates" in which information is made available over time, there is less interest in providing all information at once in order to get to an LOI, which ends Phase 2. Today's CIMs usually have enough information that allows a potential purchaser to determine whether or not they want to spend the time and money to learn more but not so much as to share the seller's "secret sauce." Second, PowerPoint presentations have become the preferred means of conveying information at this early stage. It allows the seller to quickly and easily communicate the strengths—and challenges—of the company being sold to interested parties.

A typical CIM would include things such as the following:

- The name of the company and the products or services it offers
- The company's geographic region and reach (local, national, international)

- High-level details about the company's financials for the past and future years, including revenue, expenses, and level of profitability
- An understanding as to the company's strengths and challenges
- Description of the customer base and whether those customers are project based or recurring
- An explanation of why the company is on the market (retirement, owner seeking new challenges, need for additional capital) and if the owner is willing to stay with the company after the transaction

After the CIM is completed, a one- or two-page document, called a *teaser*, is prepared. Unlike the CIM, which provides some real detail, the teaser does not disclose the identity of the selling company and should be drafted so that a reader of the teaser cannot determine the identity of the seller. The teaser should describe the selling company at a very high level. For example, a teaser might say that the seller is a construction services firm operating in the Midwest and serving the commercial market, with approximately $15 million in revenue with 10 percent margins.

At the end of this book, there is a dynamic QR code. That QR code will lead you to a model CIM.

PREPARING TO GO TO MARKET

There are two final items that need to be prepared before outreach begins to buyers.

First, the seller needs to have a nondisclosure agreement (NDA), which can be sent to potential buyers to ensure the confidentiality of the information provided. A lawyer should be involved in preparing, or at least reviewing, the NDA. No truly confidential information should be shared with potential buyers without having an executed NDA in place.

Next, there needs to be a list of potential buyers (see chapter 7). Who will the seller reach out to? Will it be strategic buyers, PE, or searchers? A list (or multiple lists) must be created that identifies the potential buyer, the specific person to whom the outreach is made, and the contact information for that person. Internet research on each buyer should be conducted to see if they have a good reputation or have been involved in litigation involving past acquisition or to spot any red flags.

A system has to be developed to track the outreach—often, more than one outreach is required—which potential buyers expressed interest, whether an NDA has been signed, and what materials have been shared.

Now, and only now, can the seller begin to reach out to potential buyers.

PHASE 2: BUYER IDENTIFICATION

The marketing process begins by sending the teaser to potential buyers or lawyers, commercial bankers, accountants, and M&A professionals who may know of potential buyers. Again, the teaser is simply a means of determining whether the recipient is interested in potentially acquiring a company of the kind described.

Response rates vary by the category of buyer. Strategic buyers usually have the lowest response rate; 3 to 5 percent is typical. Most strategic buyers are in the business of running their companies and are not necessarily looking for an acquisition. In contrast, buyers that are in the business of buying companies, such as PE and searchers, are far more responsive; if the outreach list is appropriately researched and prepared, a response rate can be as high as 20 percent.

A potential buyer response is along the lines of "I would like to learn more, including the identity of the seller." At that point, the potential buyer is sent the approved NDA. Often, the buyer wants to negotiate some of the terms of the NDA; this is not unusual and should not raise a concern. If you have any doubts about the changes the buyer wants to make to the NDA, your attorney should be involved. After the terms of the NDA have been agreed upon and the document is signed, the CIM can be shared.

After the terms of the NDA have been agreed upon and the document is signed, the CIM can be shared.

At my firm, before sharing the CIM, we take another look at the buyer. Is this a competitor to the seller? Does the potential buyer appear to have the resources to close a transaction? What is the possibility that the buyer is simply a tire kicker (see chapter 3)? We work closely with our sellers to make sure that we're not casually sharing information. We jointly determine who is going to sign an NDA and who is going to receive a CIM. As the seller, you know your marketplace. You know who has a good reputation and who doesn't. So be careful with whom you share your information.

Keep in mind there is a certain amount of information "leakage" that *will* occur regardless of the NDA or how careful you are. Moreover, the longer the process takes, the higher the likelihood of disclosure.

Fortunately, rumors about what company is on the market are so frequently wrong that you shouldn't worry too much. If someone asks you if your company is on the market, then have a standard answer like "We would sell our company tomorrow for $100 million. Are you interested?" If the issue comes up, your reaction is more important than the question. The goal is to find a buyer, which means the CIM has to be shared to move forward.

DISCUSSIONS WITH POTENTIAL BUYERS

Once potential buyers have reviewed the CIM, some will not be interested in going forward. Don't be offended; the teaser truly is a sales document. The CIM should be the place where the strengths and weaknesses of your company are outlined at a high level. For example, if your company has customer concentration or high annual capital expenditures, this information will be clear in the CIM, not the teaser. If a buyer cannot accept the customer concentration, or only wants a "cap-ex" light company, then let the buyer move on.

I advise my clients that the goal with buyers is to "fail fast." We don't want to keep buyers at the table who are not truly interested. Don't waste your time with buyers who are not enthusiastic and certainly do not share more information than is required.

Fail fast takes more discipline than you would think. At the beginning, both buyer and seller are excited, and the future seems bright. The purchaser lets the seller know how impressive the seller's business is and how terrific of a fit the seller will be with the purchaser. However, the seller needs to stay alert for statements or behavior by the purchaser that may indicate that all is not well. Here are a few items that should trigger seller concerns:

- *Comment from Purchaser:* "We are rethinking the purchase price due to current economic headwinds." This means that external events are causing the buyer to rethink whether they want to move forward.

- *Comment from Purchaser:* "We are reexamining the valuation based upon your company's recent financial performance." This means that the buyer is rethinking the purchase offer.
- *Inaction from Purchaser:* Purchaser's counsel is silent on when the purchase agreement will be forthcoming. This means that the buyer is unsure they want to move forward with the transaction.

Failing fast avoids this problem. The goal is to save the seller a tremendous amount of time, energy, and money by realizing when a potential buyer is not the right partner. The seller can then continue to focus on growing the business and finding the right buyer who will complete the acquisition.

There will be buyers who review the CIM and are interested in learning more, and there are many different approaches to this next step. Very often, buyers will provide written questions to the seller, which the seller answers in writing. Other sellers will open all or some of the data room to the potential buyer.

As an M&A advisor, I believe that discussion is the next step. My team will have a phone call or video conference with the potential buyer and reiterate the "story" of the seller. We are also interested in the "story" of the buyer, and we want to know as much as possible to determine if the buyer is credible. What is the buyer seeking to achieve by buying a company? What are their concerns? Have they ever completed an acquisition before? What is their source of capital? What do they know about the industry? If this discussion goes well, we will open a limited amount of the data room to the potential buyer.

The goal, once again, is to fail fast. We are looking to provide information that is relevant to a go/no-go decision without giving highly confidential information, such as the identity of employees or customers (assuming this is confidential).

After the potential buyer has done enough work to make a reasonable judgment and is interested in moving forward, we will arrange a direct communication between the potential buyer and the seller. (Obviously, if you are not using an M&A advisor, then you as the seller have been spending a lot of time getting to this stage.) A call between the potential buyer and the seller is called a "management meeting." There will be many management meetings before an LOI is signed. The opportunities for miscommunications are great, and the seller should have an experienced advisor participate in management meetings.

The management meeting is important, not only to share information about your company and learn about the buyer but also to determine whether there is a culture match. If you have a company where you and your employees consider yourselves "family," a buyer focused on employee productivity metrics and who sees staff as interchangeable is probably not a good fit.

While Phase 1 is preparing to go on dates, Phase 2 is actually dating. This is the time you determine whether the specific person or team in front of you is someone you feel comfortable with, whether they share your values and outlook, and whether they are seeking to achieve the same goals. Sometimes you know on a first date; sometimes it takes more time. Both the potential buyer and the seller should ask a lot of questions and listen deeply to the answers.

As a seller, you need to understand what this buyer is looking to do with your company and whether those plans make sense to you. When the buyer is getting more serious, you will begin providing more information, and more of the data room will be opened.

Once the potential buyer has a realistic view of your company, it is time to move on the LOI. You may be dealing with only one potential buyer, or you may have multiple interested parties. While having more than one suitor is gratifying, it can sometimes be complicated to juggle. But it is a good problem to have.

The potential buyer(s) should submit an LOI. An LOI is a two- to six-page agreement specifying the basic commercial terms of the acquisition. It contains the following:

- The purchase price and underlying assumptions to reach that purchase price
- The structure for paying the seller
- Amount of cash at close
- Seller financing
- Equity rollover
- Earnout
- The structure of the transaction, such as a stock or an equity acquisition
- Whether there is a financing contingency
- Length of time for the exclusivity period and scope of that exclusivity
- Projected closing date

Upon receiving an LOI (or multiple LOIs), sellers should ask the potential buyer to review the document together. There are often mistakes in an LOI, and the language does not reflect what the buyer meant. It is far better to clearly understand what the buyer was trying to accomplish than take the words on the page as gospel. If the LOI is clear, great! But this is the time to begin the mantra of "no assumptions." Assumptions are often where transactions go wrong. Clarity of communication without judgment, anger, or frustration is critically important from this point to the closing … and beyond.

Negotiations regarding the LOI can take a week, a month, or even longer. Each transaction is different, but in most cases the negotiations take several weeks.

Sellers will often bring one or two trusted employees into a small circle of people who know about the transaction and can speak with the buyer. Some sellers do not allow any employees to be informed about the transaction. This is a fact-specific question and usually discussed between the buyer and the seller for both the pre-LOI and post-LOI period. The buyer should not assume they will have contact with any employees without getting specific agreement from the seller.

Both the buyer and the seller should engage their own lawyer to review the LOI before signing. Even if the LOI seems clear, I urge you to have a lawyer—and probably your accountant—review it before execution of the agreement. There are some legal and accounting provisions that can have an impact on your company *and* the transaction. This is a good time to be humble and get professional advice.

When signed, the LOI signifies that the parties are engaged, not married. While the LOI is generally nonbinding, it is an extremely important document. In the LOI, the seller commits to "exclusivity"; they will take the company off the market for a specific time period, usually ninety days. There's no more dating during the exclusivity period. The buyer has that time period to complete due diligence, get

Only sign the LOI if you would be happy to close on the terms outlined therein.

legal documents drafted and negotiated, and obtain financing to purchase the seller. Exclusivity is required so the buyer feels comfortable spending money on due diligence, lawyers, and bank commitment fees.

A word of caution: Only sign the LOI if you would be happy to close on the terms outlined therein. You shouldn't get engaged unless you plan to marry.

LOIs come in many forms. At the end of this book, there is a dynamic QR code. That QR code will lead you to a model LOI, but be flexible. LOIs come in all shapes and sizes. The LOI you receive from a buyer may be very different. Make sure your attorney thoroughly reviews the LOI with you before signing.

PHASE 3: LOI TO CLOSING

MAINTAIN CONFIDENTIALITY AFTER THE LOI

I was selling a manufacturing company on behalf of a client to a PE firm. Immediately after signing the LOI, and without telling me, the seller had a company-wide meeting to announce the execution of the LOI and the plan to sell the company. This was not a great idea. We spent the next three weeks answering questions and preventing star employees from jumping ship.

Employees get nervous when they hear about a possible transaction. They wonder,

- "Am I going to get fired?"
- "Will my salary or benefits be reduced?"
- "Who am I going to be reporting to?"
- "How will things change?"

The truth is, immediately after signing the LOI, you will not have real answers for any of these questions. As a result, calming employees is exceedingly difficult. By telling employees immediately after signing the LOI, you have raised emotional and financial issues without the means to quiet their concerns.

Signing an LOI does not mean the transaction will close. As I tell anyone who will listen, no deal is done until the money crosses the wire. A signed LOI is an important step in that direction, but there are many off-ramps before closing. And the worst situation to be in is to tell employees about a transaction that does not occur.

That does not mean you don't inform any employees. There may be an individual or two that you bring into the inner circle post-LOI. There should be a specific reason for sharing this information, and you must ensure they can maintain the confidence.

There are two main reasons to inform a select employee or two. First, this person might be extremely helpful in responding to extensive post-LOI due diligence requests. These are not only financial; I have seen sellers bring business development staff into the circle to help the buyer understand future opportunities. Second, trust is a two-way street. It is hard to get employees to trust you if you expressly show that you do not trust them. I've witnessed many hurt feelings when an employee, who has worked with the seller for decades, is not given special status by informing them of the transaction before a general employee announcement.

You also determine when to inform these one or two people. It could be immediately after LOI or in the week or two prior to closing. There is no firm and fast rule. Use your judgment (and discuss with your advisors) to best balance the need to maintain confidentiality, respond to detailed due diligence requests by the buyer, and maintain valued relationships.

CLOSING TIMELINE - OVERVIEW

KEY TASKS	PROJECTED 11-WEEK SCHEDULE										
X/XX: Signed LOI	WK1	WK2	WK3	WK4	WK5	WK6	WK7	WK8	WK9	WK10	WK11
Phase III: Preparation[1] and Kick-Off Meeting w/ Seller and Buyer	●										
Processing Due Diligence List Information[2]		███	███	███	███						
Definitive Agreement First Draft			███	███							
QofE Process & Deliverable				███	███	███					
Negotiate Legal Documents[3]						███	███	███	███		
NWC Calculation and Agreement							███	███			
Complete Closing Checklist								███	███		
DEAL CLOSING TARGET											●

[1] Includes sbLiftOff responsibilities for (virtual) Data Room, Working Group List, and review of process with Seller

[2] May include 3rd party due diligence work streams such as insurance/benefits/retirement, accounting, legal, IT, environmental, and background checks

[3] Includes Stock Purchase Agreement (SPA), Lease Agreements, Disclosure Schedules, and Net Working Capital (NWC) methodology

SELLER HIGHEST PRICE IS NOW BUT WILL CHANGE

The price in the LOI is the high point for the seller. I have never been involved in a transaction where the buyer said, "We have learned such wonderful things about your company during post-LOI due diligence that we would like to pay you an additional 10 percent."

The buyer is looking to justify the purchase price and determine if they are overpaying. The presumption is that unless something materially different is found about the seller post-LOI, the transaction will close at the LOI purchase price. An ethical buyer does not try to nickel-and-dime a seller with small items post-LOI, although some of that is to be expected in any human-run organization. But if the buyer discovers an unexpected situation that significantly reduces the value of the company, it could lead to a price reduction and ill will among the parties. Even without price adjustments, you will be required to absorb some expenses that were not included in your budget. It could be paying off accrued vacation for employees, upgrading your cybersecurity system, paying more for net working capital, dealing with a tax issue, or a myriad of other items.

I advocate the 97 percent rule. When I was a kid in school, my goal was to get 97 percent on a test. If I got 100, that was fantastic. But 97 was excellent, and I would be satisfied. The 97 percent rule applies to selling your company. If you get 97 percent of the purchase price shown on the LOI, that is a win. Don't put this at risk to gain an additional 3 percent.

Here's an example. I had a client that was a cutting-edge technology company with a large, talented, and highly credentialed staff. The purchaser was a strategic and eager to pay twice the valuation that the financials supported. A dispute arose over whether the buyer or the seller should be responsible for paying out $150,000 of vacation benefits to employees. My client, truly a brilliant man, became frustrated and yelled, "We are not going to pay for this, and if the buyer continues to push, we will not do this sale!" I asked him to tell me what percentage of the sales price this $150,000 represented. He stopped, thought for a moment, and concluded that it was less than one-half of 1 percent. That helped him put the issue in perspective; this was a small issue.

Be prepared because there will be costs for which you are unprepared. You will not win all issues that arise after the LOI. Be happy with 97 percent.

MORE DUE DILIGENCE

The biggest step in Phase 3 is more due diligence. Although the seller should have provided extensive data to the buyer before signing the LOI, the buyer will engage in deeper review. For many items, the post-LOI due diligence is when the buyer tests and ensures all that has been said pre-LOI is accurate. This is when it pays off for the seller to have provided the buyer with extensive information prior to signing the LOI. If the seller has accurately provided the strengths and challenges of the company, the buyer's due diligence is "confirmatory," meaning that the company is as represented pre-LOI. However, if the seller has concealed problems, the buyer is likely to discover them during post-LOI due diligence.

Upon learning of the previously undisclosed problem, the buyer thinks either of the following:

- Did the seller not know of this problem? If they didn't know, then what else don't they know about their company? I no longer trust that the seller has control over this company. I might be buying a mess. The riskiness of this transaction just increased, so I may need to reduce the price.

- Did the seller know of this problem and not tell me? If they knew and didn't tell me, what other problems exist that they didn't tell me? I no longer trust the honesty of the seller. The riskiness of this transaction just increased, so I may need to reduce the price.

If the discovery is material, whether the lack of disclosure was intentional or not, the result is often an adjustment to the terms of the LOI, particularly price. This is a bad result for all the parties but particularly the seller, who could have avoided this result.

Some sellers think they can hide problems until after closing. This is a bad strategy. First, the likelihood is that the problem will be discovered during the post-LOI due diligence.[19] Second, as part of the transaction, the seller makes many "representations and warranties" (R&W) about the company. A problem discovered after closing is likely to create a breach of these R&Ws, and the seller will have to pay the buyer for that breach. (At closing, the seller usually funds an escrow account to cover breaches of the R&Ws). It is far better to be honest and forthcoming than to try to game the system.

At the end of this book, there is a dynamic QR code. That QR code will lead you to a model due diligence check list.

LEGAL DOCUMENTS

There are a shocking number of legal and commercial documents needed to close the sale. The key document is the purchase agreement in which ownership transfers from the seller to the buyer. While the LOI is approximately five pages, the purchase agreement is usually sixty to one hundred pages, depending on the structure and complexity of the transaction.

---

19   Due diligence is detailed in chapter 10.

The longest section in the purchase agreement is the R&W made by the seller. These R&Ws include statements such as the company compliance with specific laws and regulations, paid taxes, disclosure of past litigation, details of benefit plans, lists of insurance policies, and many other items.

Disclosure schedules are then prepared and attached to the purchase agreement to ensure accuracy. For instance, the purchase agreement might state that the company has not had any litigation other than what is listed in the disclosure schedules. The disclosure schedule would then list past litigation to ensure the R&W is accurate.

Completing the purchase agreement and preparing the disclosure schedules is a heavy lift and takes time. At the end of this book, there is a dynamic QR code. That QR code will lead you to a model Table of Contents for a Purchase Agreement. Legal expenses add up fast. Frequently, the buyer will want to complete key areas of due diligence before authorizing lawyers to begin drafting documents. This is not surprising, but there should be discussions between the buyer and the seller prior to signing the LOI to understand the buyer's plans for preparation of legal documents.

SETTING NET WORK CAPITAL TARGET

During Phase 3, the parties discuss and agree upon a net working capital (NWC) target. Outside the purchase price—and the payment structure to the seller—NWC is among the most contentious issues in a transaction. NWC is the difference between current assets and current liabilities. To simplify for the purpose of explanation but not accuracy, it is the difference between accounts receivable (A/R) and accounts payable (A/P).

In addition to being profitable, a successful company must have the ability to pay its bills when due. This liquidity is the "oil" in the gears of the machine that allows it to function. NWC is this liquidity. It is an asset of the company that gets transferred from the seller to the buyer at close.

In the best situation, NWC is provided when the seller transfers the balance sheet to the buyer. The key elements on the transferred balance sheet are the A/R and the A/P. The buyer needs to ensure that enough A/R will convert into cash to pay the obligations of the A/P on time.

Here is a sample balance sheet over a six-month period:

A/R	$950K	$725K	$875K	$1.05M	$900K	$650K
A/P	$700K	$650K	$750K	$980K	$790K	$500K
NWC	$250K	$75K	$125K	$70K	$110K	$150K

Note that the NWC varies each month. The end of each month is simply a snapshot of the A/R and A/P at that moment in time. Also, note that the NWC for month one is more than three times the NWC for month four. So how do you decide how much NWC the seller must provide the buyer?

In most circumstances, the parties decide on a time period to calculate a target NWC. In the case above, the average NWC for the six-month period is $130,000; the average NWC for the three-month period is $110,000. The buyer and the seller—and their many advisors—need to negotiate which of these averages to use as the target NWC, which must be delivered by the seller at close.

Here is the key to setting a target NWC: It should not be a purchase price adjustment in favor of the seller or the buyer. Each side should be determining what the buyer will need to run the company for the thirty days or so after the acquisition.

Books have been written on determining NWC, and this is just a light touch on this issue. There can be a complex set of adjustments to NWC, and the negotiations can be intense. Remember, this is not a time to try to gain an advantage over the other side. If you keep the purpose of NWC in mind during the negotiation, the process will be smoother than if either side is trying to benefit in the NWC calculation.

WHY CLOSING MATTERS

During the negotiations, there is constant talk about the "closing." What is the closing, and why does it matter? What happens at the closing?

The closing is the moment when ownership transfers from seller to buyer. Closing is when all the documents have been signed, the signature pages exchanged, escrows created, all lines of credit closed, liens removed, and so many other details have been prepared, reviewed, and accepted by both sides. The parties agree that the transaction is closed, and the buyer initiates the wire transfers. As a reminder, no deal is done until the money crosses the wire.

> **The closing is the moment when ownership transfers from seller to buyer... It is the big bang moment.**

The closing is the big bang moment, and any liabilities that exist in that moment belong to the seller. Any new liabilities belong to the buyer.

Sellers sometimes mistakenly think that when they transfer their companies, they transfer existing problems. Generally, that is not the case. If you are fighting with the IRS or defending a lawsuit, that issue will not disappear when you sell your company and will continue to be your problem. However, you shouldn't incur any new liabilities from your company going forward.

At the end of this book, there is a dynamic QR code. That QR code will lead you to a model Contents for a Closing Binder.

POSTCLOSING

For the seller, closing eases the burden of the transaction, but some responsibilities remain.

The first goal is to determine who needs to be told of the transaction and what needs to be communicated. Employees are typically informed of the transaction but not the purchase price or the structure.

Some buyers want customers and vendors to know about the sale, but others do not. This is truly a discussion point between the parties. I have witnessed buyers wait for months before making an announcement. By the time the customer knows of the change, they have already experienced working with the new team. The communications plan is discussed during Phase 3 but implemented upon the close.

The seller may also work for the buyer after the transaction. I have been involved in transition periods as short as three weeks and as long as several years. Again, this is a point of negotiation between the parties. As the seller, it is difficult to go from boss to employee. Keep your ego in check. Your goal is to help the buyer be successful.

Two to four months after closing, there is an NWC "true-up." The seller prepares a balance sheet as of the closing, and NWC is delivered at close. In virtually all cases, the balance sheet cannot accurately capture all the expenses, income, or adjustments required, so the parties wait a few months to create an accurate balance sheet as of the closing date. Upon the new balance sheet, NWC delivered is recalculated, and there may be funds owed from or due to the seller. This true-up is important, and most sellers include their advisors in this process.

One to two years after the closing, most of the representation and warranties made by the seller in the purchase document terminate.

There may be claims that the buyer has for breaches of the reps and warranties, which is not unusual and often the subject of negotiation between the parties.

The following is an outline of the postclosing activities in most transactions:

POST PHASE 3

DESCRIP-TION	TIMELINE POST-CLOSING*	BUYER ROLE/ IMPACT	SELLER ROLE/ IMPACT
Transaction Announcement	<1 Week	Communicates Transaction Benefits and Implications to Employees, Customers, and Vendors	
Final NWC True Up Final vs. Est. Closing	2–3 Months	Produces Final Closing Balance Sheet	Validates/Reconciles Buyer's Final Closing Balance Sheet
NWC Escrow	<6 Months	Retains or Releases (Contingent on TrueUp)	Withheld from Purchase Price (Contingent on TrueUp)
R&W Escrow	18–24 Months	Retains or Releases (Contingent on Claims)	Withheld from Purchase Price (Contingent on Claims)
Seller Transition	1 Month– 2 Years	Knowledge Transfer + Succession Planning	Employment agreement (if applicable)
Post-Merger Integration	6–12 Months	Implements Go Forward Systems, Accounting, HR, Benefits, Org. Chart, etc.	Knowledge Transfer + Advisory Capacity

LIFT OFF LESSONS

- Selling a company can be understood in the following three basic phases:
    - □ Phase 1: Preparation
    - □ Phase 2: Buyer Identification
    - □ Phase 3: LOI to Closing
- Preparation is required for a good transfer. Preparation, preparation, preparation is the mantra of most M&A professionals, and it's wise to begin preparation even years prior to sale.
- In Phase 1, the "story of the company" and the basic sales documents, such as the blind teaser and the CIM, are created.
- In Phase 2, the company goes to market while maintaining confidentiality.
- As qualified buyers are considered, it is important that sellers do their due diligence on buyers, and buyers do their due diligence on the seller.
- The LOI acts as an "engagement ring." Both parties are signifying that they are intending to move forward with the transaction on these terms.
- With the signing of the LOI, more power goes to the buyer, and Phase 3 starts, which is known as the "rush to close."
- Phase 3 will include a lot more due diligence, but if it's *confirmatory*, price adjustments will not occur.
- Time kills deals. While these phases are time-consuming, it is important that the deal move forward in a professional manner and to an expeditious close.

CHAPTER 9

HOW MUCH WILL THIS COST?

I can't tell you how many times I've had sellers of companies ask, "How much will this cost?" What the seller is really asking is, "How much will I put in my pocket?" The answer is an emphatic … "It depends."

The place to start is by asking, "Is my company *ready* to be sold?" Let's go back to our analogy of selling a house.

When selling your home, there are usually costs to prepare your house to be listed. They might be major costs such as replacing the roof, repainting the exterior, replacing windows, or installing new floors. Some houses only need minor repairs or maintenance, such as cleaning carpets, emptying closets, or sprucing up landscaping. But there is always some cost involved to get a house ready for sale.

The goal is for potential buyers to say "Wow, this is a great house!" You want buyers to envision themselves living in your house and feeling good about purchasing it.

Once the house is on the market, there are no significant costs until the house is under contract to a buyer. To close the sale, you will need to hire an attorney, pay any accrued but unpaid taxes, and pay your real estate agent.

Selling your company is analogous to selling a house. Before going to market, you have to prepare for a deep review of all aspects of your company. In some cases, records are so poor that an accountant must be retained to recreate years of financial statements and ensure accuracy. The financial records must provide information, not raise questions.

You might be saying, "I'm 100 percent certain that my financial house is in order."

Congratulations! You are steps ahead of many founders/owners. In your case, make sure your financial records have been reviewed by a third party such as an accountant, a lawyer, or an M&A advisor. Again, the goal is to ensure that the records are clear to someone other than the seller.

This is also the time to determine whether you have nonsolicitation/noncompete agreements with certain employees. Your company is more valuable if there are employees (outside of ownership) who play a major role in operating the company. A buyer will want to know that, upon a sale, those employees will not immediately leave, taking other employees or customers with them.

If there are any employees whom you are particularly concerned about losing or whom you want to reward, some sellers provide select employees with a *change of control* agreement. As noted in Deepak Malhotra's article titled "Control the Negotiation before It Begins" for the *Harvard Business Review*,[20]

---

20   Deepak Malhotra, "Control the Negotiation before It Begins," December 2015, https://hbr.org/2015/12/control-the-negotiation-before-it-begins.

Countless books and articles offer advice on avoiding missteps at the bargaining table. But some of the costliest mistakes take place before negotiators sit down to discuss the substance of the deal.

That's because they often take for granted that if they bring a lot of value to the table and have sufficient leverage, they'll be able to strike a great deal. While negotiating from a position of strength is certainly important, many other factors influence where each party ends up.

A change of control agreement allows certain employees to either terminate or adjust their terms of employment, such as payment, bonuses, paid time off, etc., upon a change of structure or ownership. Under this agreement, if there is a change of control, the employee receives some type of bonus compensation. Smart owners ensure that employees with change of control agreements need to stay with the company after a transaction for six to twenty-four months to collect this bonus.

■ ■ ■

The costs in Phase 1 are entirely dependent upon your company's readiness to be scrutinized by potential buyers and their advisors.

During Phase 2, when your company is being marketed, the costs are minimal. There might be some travel costs and, strangely enough, restaurant bills. After an in-person management meeting, the buyer and the seller often go to lunch or dinner. (For some reason, these meals tend to be in steakhouses, an expensive option.) These meals can add up, if there are a lot of potential buyers. While this is a unique expense, it's also a very important one.

Unlike selling a home, where the buyer and the seller rarely cross paths, in the sale of a business, the seller and the buyer will meet each other. They have to see if there's a culture match, whether there's a commonality of vision as to what the company is and what it should be, how to treat employees, and much more. The restaurant represents a "pub" of sorts that creates an informal let's-get-to-know-each-other atmosphere. Certainly, the buyer and the seller have meetings in dull conference rooms and talk about all sorts of business details. But at a restaurant they get together to determine the following: Do I like this person? Is this someone I could work with? Is this somebody who I think can take on my company and do with it what I think needs to be done? As the host, the seller usually picks up the bill. Certainly, buyers occasionally offer, which is nice but not the norm.

Phase 3—LOI to close—is where expenses ramp up.

LAWYER FEES

In Phase 1, the lawyer should review (or produce) the NDA that is used, which is a minor expense. In Phase 2, make sure your lawyer reviews the LOI before you sign. This is a modest expense. Phase 3, LOI to close, is when lawyer expenses are significant.

Please use a lawyer who is an experienced M&A attorney.

Legal fees for the seller can vary greatly depending upon the size and complexity of the transaction and the lawyer retained. For a $10 million purchase price transaction, the fee could be a low of $75,000 or a high of hundreds of thousands of dollars. I once saw a buyer incur $2 million in legal fees on a $34 million acquisition. (I thought this was insane.)

This is where I get on my soapbox and say, "Please use a lawyer who is an experienced M&A attorney. Don't use your brother-in-law who did your trust and estate or the guy down the street that you like." There are so many details in selling your company, and it is imperative to have experienced counsel.

There are excellent M&A lawyers at large law firms. Unfortunately, these firms tend to be pretty expensive. Sometimes you can find lawyers who are equally experienced and cost materially less. But don't go for lower cost with less experience.

If you're having heart bypass surgery, you want to use a surgeon who's done the procedure ten thousand times, not someone who is doing their third procedure. Getting an experienced M&A attorney, preferably one who knows your industry, is very important. While it might seem more expensive, it will save you money in the long term.

In addition to experience, you need to have a lawyer that you trust. This will become a personal relationship—at least during the transaction—so make sure your lawyer is someone with whom you are comfortable.

In most transactions, each side pays its own legal fees. These fees are not contingent and are due even if the transaction does not close.

ACCOUNTING FEES

You will incur accounting fees relating to tax issues and determination of the NWC. It's also a good idea to have your accountant review the LOI before you sign it. In total, accounting fees will be $10,000–$40,000, depending upon the firm you use and the complexity of the issues.

When spending money on accountants, don't be penny wise and pound foolish, as the saying goes.

In most transactions, each side pays its own accounting fees. These fees are not contingent and are due even if the transaction does not close.

TAIL INSURANCE

You may not have heard of tail insurance, so I'll explain. When you own your company, you probably have insurance, whether it's liability, cyber, or errors and omissions. Upon selling your company, these policies will terminate.

Let's say you've had a professional liability insurance policy for ten years prior to a close. Six months after close, you and the company are sued for professional malpractice relating to an incident that occurred two years prior. While that claim would be covered by insurance if the policy was still active, because the policy has been terminated, there is no coverage.

Tail insurance gives your business protection for claims that are reported *after* your insurance policy ends. It will continue to ensure your business for the period that was covered in the past but for claims that come up in the future.

Most buyers require sellers to purchase tail coverage for claims that arise years after the closing.

A seller could say, "I'm willing to take that risk. I will self-insure." However, buyers don't want sellers to take that risk. If a claim arises, the buyer has to get reimbursed from the seller, which can be awkward and difficult. It's better to pursue a normal insurance route.

Depending upon the company and the type of insurance, tail insurance usually costs between $15,000 and $40,000. This is a cost for the seller alone but is not incurred unless the transaction closes.

REPS AND WARRANTIES ESCROW

The reps and warranties escrow comes as a surprise to many sellers. In the best of worlds, all of the funds in the escrow are eventually returned to the seller, but this escrow is usually a reduction to cash at close.

When a buyer purchases a company, the largest section of the purchase agreement is what's referred to as "representations and warranties." The seller is saying things such as, "We've paid our taxes, we don't have any litigation, we don't have any employee claims, and we've been in compliance with all laws." Exceptions to these broad assertions are listed in *disclosure schedules* that are attached to the purchase agreement.

The reps and warranties escrow is the buyer's way of saying, "It's all very nice that you're committing to these things, but what if you're wrong? What if you didn't tell me something or you didn't know about it?" Typically, somewhere between 7 and 15 percent of the purchase price goes into an escrow account that is essentially an insurance policy for the buyer. Any costs incurred by the buyer resulting from a breach of reps and warranties can be recovered from this escrow. The reps and warranties escrow generally gets released (i.e., the funds are returned to the seller) twelve to twenty-four months after the transaction closes.

The percentage of the escrow and the timing for its release are negotiated between the buyer and the seller.

As a reminder, if seller financing is being used in a transaction, the parties can negotiate a reduction or elimination of the reps and warranties escrow. The buyer has the right to recover its claims through reductions to seller financing.

NET WORKING CAPITAL

Net working capital (NWC) is the "oil" in the gears that makes the company work. It is also one of the most hotly negotiated and confusing aspects of a company sale. NWC is discussed in chapter 8.

Because it is difficult to have an accurate balance sheet on the day of close, the parties usually agree to an NWC escrow in case the seller owes the buyer more funds on an NWC true-up.

An escrow for NWC is usually terminated 60–120 days after closing. Nonetheless, this escrow is a reduction of cost at closing for which the seller should be prepared.

M&A ADVISOR

Chapter 12 details why you should retain an M&A advisor, so I will not repeat these reasons here.

Unlike your lawyer or accountant, the M&A advisor's compensation is largely contingent upon closing the transaction. That means there is an alignment of interests between the seller and the M&A advisor. The M&A fee is usually a percentage of the purchase price in the purchase agreement (often with a minimum fee). Fees range as high as 12 percent, with higher percentages attributed with acquisitions of smaller companies.

PURCHASE PRICE	M&A ADVISOR FEE
Under $1 million	10-12 percent
$1 million to $5 million	6-10 percent
$5 million to $10 million	5-6 percent
$10 million and above	Varies

Smaller companies pay higher percentages because the time and effort to close a $3 million deal is typically just as great as what is required for a $30 million deal. The due diligence is just as extensive and the legal documents just as numerous and individually negotiated in the smaller deal than the larger one. In fact, there are times when a $3 million deal is more complicated because the seller is often more emotionally involved; there may be more "art" than "science" in valuation of smaller companies.

MISCELLANEOUS EXPENSES

Remember, these transactions are done as debt free/cash free. In addition to traditional debt that you have already considered—lines of credit, term bank loans, etc.—there may be liabilities on the company that you haven't thought about. The most common is accrued but unpaid vacation for employees. This expense can add up.

I had a client who was proud that his employees were so dedicated to the company that they rarely took vacation. In response to my question of whether this unused vacation was accrued, he smiled and said, "Of course." In fact, two employees had been with his company so long and had taken so little vacation that they had over fifty-two weeks of accrued vacation. When we sold his company, there was a payout of over $600,000 to employees for this liability.

While some buyers may be willing to accept unpaid vacation as a liability on the company for NWC purposes, most buyers want this paid to employees at closing. In fact, some states have requirements that citizens of their states must receive cash in their circumstances. The smart seller assumes this will need to be paid off.

Before you go to market, preferably a year or so in advance, look at your employee vacation policy. Many companies now have a use-it-or-lose-it vacation policy or limit unused vacation time rollover to one or two weeks. Adopting these policies before going to market can save you a lot of money when you decide to sell.

Another issue relates to employee bonuses. Even though most companies pay employee bonuses on a discretionary basis, a buyer will want to ensure that employees receive the same bonus after close that they would have received if there had been no transfer. The buyer often asks the seller to fund the bonus for the time period the seller held the company.

For instance, let's assume that $600,000 in bonuses were paid in the year preceding the sale of the company. If the company is transferred on October 31, the buyer is likely to ask the seller to pay $500,000 toward the bonuses that will be paid to employees in December. This is a heavily negotiated point.

Another often forgotten expense is prorated income taxes. Just because taxes are not yet payable does not mean they have not been accruing. The seller is responsible for all income taxes related to income earned prior to the transfer.

TAXES ON THE SALE

There are many tax issues associated with selling your company, and this section is not a treatise on the subject. Here are some highlight issues for you to consider and discuss with your advisors.

First, taxes are by far the biggest cost. Unlike escrows for reps and warranties or NWC, you are not going to get this money back.

Second, the profit on the sale of your business is taxed at capital gain rates, which are materially lower than ordinary income rates applicable to your company. What is the significance of that?

Let's say you sell your company for a three times EBITDA multiple, meaning that you are receiving at close the amount that you would earn over the next three years. You are in fact doing better by selling your company. You have the cash in hand today and reduced your risk of owning the company, and your purchase price will also be taxed at approximately half of what your earnings would be taxed at over those three years.

Converting income from ordinary income into capital gains is a major benefit.

The flip side? Expenses that reduce your ordinary income are better than expenses that reduce your capital gains. Be sure to work with your accountant to determine whether some portion of your legal, accounting, and other expenses can be paid in the ordinary course of business and therefore reduce ordinary income and not capital gains.

Accountants and lawyers who help you correctly allocate income to capital gains and expenses to ordinary income are valuable players on your team. Again, experience counts. Always work with advisors who know what is legitimate and what is not.

Accountants and lawyers who help minimize taxes are valuable team members.

Third, taxes are not paid on the purchase price listed in the purchase agreement but are based on the net profit.

Fourth, the sale of your company might be subject to state-level taxation as well. There is a reason why a business might leave New Jersey, with capital gains rates of over 11 percent, and reincorporate in Florida, where the capital gains rate is zero.

There are a lot of tax issues, and the more you understand, the greater your potential for saving.[21] In any event, taxes on the sale of your business will be the largest expense that reduces the amount of cash that goes into your pocket.

■ ■ ■

---

21   There may be surprising benefits. For instance, one of the best advantages for a C-corp is called "Section 1202," which allows for a very significant percentage of gains to be excluded from taxation. C-corps tend to pay more in taxes than other types of entities while they are active, and Section 1202 allows the C-corp to recoup much of that taxation.

I'm sure you can see why the answer to the question, "How much will I put in my pocket?" is an emphatic "It depends." The above costs incurred when selling a company will vary in details and amount to be paid based on each unique transaction. The key is to structure these costs so that you walk away from the sale with as much as possible and a sense of satisfaction that the deal you made is the right one for you.

TRANSACTION COSTS

ALLOCATION OF EXPENSES	PRICE RANGE	RESPONSIBILITY
Legal Fees Includes legal & tax due diligence, counsel, and document preparation	$75-250K+	Both
Accounting Includes financial and tax analyses, tax due diligence, and integration planning	$30-50K (0.25% of Purchase Price)	Both
M&A Advisory Includes Buyer/Seller search, marketing materials, due diligence, and negotiations/structuring	$30-50K (4-6% of Purchase Price)	Both
Quality of Earnings (QofE) Independent report aimed at providing accurate GAAP approved financials	$40-80K	Buyer
Tail D&O Insurance Insurance covering any claims that occurred before deal is closed	$20-40K	Seller
Additional Contingency Placeholder to cover excess costs related to more complex deal terms	$100K	Both
Total Transaction Costs*	**$665K+**	

*Escrows or holdbacks (e.g., Reps & Warranties and NWC) may also impact Seller's immediate transaction proceeds at closing.

LIFT OFF LESSONS

- There is no hard-and-fast formula for selling a company. The costs involved are variables, which will have a direct impact on how much you, the owner/founder, will pocket after the transaction is complete.
- When preparing to sell your company, be advised that a potential buyer is going to go through your financials with a fine-tooth comb.
- If there are any employees that you are particularly concerned about losing or that you want to reward, you can use a *change of control* provision to state your terms.

CHAPTER 10

WHAT IS DUE DILIGENCE?

In 2023 a story about due diligence broke that had everyone on Wall Street talking. JPMorgan Chase had paid $175 million to a young darling in the fintech startup space. Her name was Charlie Javice, and she had made headlines with an idea of helping five million college students deal with FAFSA application headaches. The allure of building a closer relationship with five million college students each year brought JPMorgan Chase and its famous CEO, Jamie Dimon, to the M&A table. But when the deal closed, the bank realized they had been "conned"—or at least that's what JPMorgan Chase's lawyers argued persuasively in court. Their filing was jaw-dropping. According to the bank's complaint, they had paid $175 million and failed to notice that the customer list was fake. The JPMorgan Chase's lawyers said the young entrepreneur had "pulled the wool over their eyes."[22]

Everyone up on Wall Street shook their heads. Imagine, the biggest bank in the United States neglecting the basics of due diligence!

As we've already discussed, there's no deal without due diligence. We've talked previously about the fact that when a buyer approaches a seller, it's important that the buyer shows empathy and respect to that seller; that person has grown and managed a profitable business. But every good deed deserves a good turn, and now, as the seller of the business, it's your turn to be an empathetic and respectful human.

UNDERSTANDING THE BUYER'S PREDICAMENT

By the time you have a buyer you think is credible and interested, it will be time to face more due diligence. During this time—which is often described by owners as "a proctology exam"—you need to understand what the other side is going through, something I call "the buyer's predicament."

On the close of the day, every seller knows more about their company than the buyer does. No matter how much due diligence has been done, you, the seller, will always know more. On the other side of the table is a person who doesn't know a lot about your company and hasn't lived it for years or gone through the good times and the bad. Sure, they have some familiarity with the company. But they're risking a lot of time and money believing this deal is a good idea, and they're nervous.

---

22   Ron Lieber, "How Charlie Javice Got JPMorgan to Pay $175 Million for… What Exactly?," nytimes.com (*The New York Times*, January 21, 2023), https://www. nytimes.com/2023/01/21/business/jpmorgan-chase-charlie-javice-fraud.html.

There's just no way out of the buyer's predicament. Due diligence is the only soothing balm, and it's one that you would turn to as well if you were going to buy a company. You would want to satisfy yourself that you had really "kicked the tires" by assessing challenges, strengths, and classic market risks. This is what your buyer will be doing in due diligence. While no one would ever tell you the due diligence process is fun, it is just part of the process—a vital part.

THE THREE PHASES OF DUE DILIGENCE

As I've noted before, there must be a reasonable amount of transparency between buyer and seller. However, it is incumbent upon both parties to do their own due diligence, which happens in three phases.

PHASE 1: PREPARATION

During Phase 1—preparation—you, the seller, should be doing due diligence on your own company. Your due diligence starts with making sure you have access to all the records for your company, and if you are missing any, then you do what is necessary to get the copies you need. Similar to selling your house, your business might need some renovations. These might include reviewing all expenses, examining accounting policies, taking a critical look at P&P, and making sure that all job positions are contributing to your company's bottom line. During this self-review it is helpful to have an experienced advisor working with you who knows what to look for, what needs to be done, and what can be left as is. Getting in that third-party viewpoint in this early preparation phase is critical. With the right advisor, you will be able to go to market with confidence, certain that your business will show well.

PHASE 2: BUYER IDENTIFICATION

During Phase 2—buyer identification—you will be assessing which buyers you like and which you do not. The buyers who are truly interested in your company will ask all sorts of questions—the same as someone who would want to buy your house. You shouldn't be offended by anything the buyer may ask, and I say this because often sellers do get offended. Don't allow yourself to get emotional and overreact to due diligence requests. The buyer needs to know your company's strengths and weaknesses, so there are no foolish questions in their mind. They'll want to satisfy themselves and calm their anxieties. In addition, the buyer will have additional stakeholders, such as bankers, who themselves have due diligence questions. These additional parties to the deal can add all kinds of requests for information.

There are two different philosophies regarding due diligence in Phase 2. Some people believe that the buyer should only get access to very high-level information prior to offering and signing an LOI. This means that the seller is essentially in a constant sales mode and talking about all the wonderful things about their company without necessarily talking about any problems.

I don't believe in that approach, and I think most of the M&A professional community is with me on this one.

Sellers should not only expect buyers to do extensive due diligence prior to an LOI; they should also *require* it.

Both seller and buyer want to sign the LOI based on reality. The seller is well served by the buyer doing real due diligence prior to the LOI. Unfortunately, sellers generally have a tendency to want to hide issues that buyers want to know about. If your company was sued by an employee a couple of years ago, the seller wants to know. Is there a current IRS audit? Did the company just lose its largest customer?

There might be information about insurance policies or benefits for employees that the seller needs to know. Every issue is important to the buyer, and the seller has an obligation to be forthcoming. This type of disclosure reaffirms trust and builds a strong relationship between the buyer and the seller. If the seller doesn't disclose things that the buyer has a legitimate interest in knowing about, the entire process becomes less stable. The last thing either the seller or the buyer wants to happen is for an undisclosed problem to surface at the last minute that could lead to renegotiating the LOI.

PHASE 3: LOI TO CLOSING

During Phase 3—LOI to closing—all of the remaining due diligence should be *confirmatory*. If you, the seller, and your team of experts have done your job correctly, the buyer should not be finding things that are entirely new or surprising. The buyer wants to verify that what you told them throughout the selling process to this point is, in fact, true. The buyer's checklist could be four to seven pages, but here is a caveat: many of the questions included in the checklist might be not applicable, but they will still need to be answered. For example, what intellectual property was created? What tax liens have ever existed on the company, even if they're resolved? While the answers might be "not applicable," the buyer still needs reassurance regarding any issue they might be concerned about or their financing partner might phrase.

The phrase "trust, but verify" sums up due diligence in this period.

HOW FULL DISCLOSURE BUILDS TRUST AND COOPERATION

Overall, the M&A process is an exercise in trust. The seller takes the first step toward the buyer, then the buyer takes their step. It is a cautious methodology, and the parties don't jump into "celebration mode" immediately. As I've stated, honesty and authenticity are the best policy for every step, so trust is integral throughout the business sale transaction.

On a personal level, if a couple was to get engaged, then one person found out their fiancé(e) had been in jail for three years, that surprise would cause the unsuspecting person to seriously rethink whether or not to go forward with the relationship. Conversely, if the seller's company had serious legal issues, even from the past, it is better to disclose this information; otherwise, trust and confidence between the parties can quickly be eroded.

I was the M&A advisor for sale in which the buyer looked very compatible to the seller. After the LOI was signed, we were negotiating the terms of the deal when it was disclosed that the buyer was having trouble getting financing. I didn't understand why because the economics worked for both parties. Only then did the buyer disclose that they had previously filed for bankruptcy. The problem wasn't that the buyer didn't disclose this to the seller; the problem was the buyer never disclosed this information to the bank that was involved. While the bank had preapproved the financing, finding out about the bankruptcy was a huge hurdle, even though it had happened fifteen years earlier. The bank finally said, "We don't think we can work with this guy," and the deal fell apart.

Honesty and authenticity are always the best policy.

A couple of years later, that same buyer was bidding on another company that I was involved with. Obviously, I knew about the bankruptcy, so I was much more diligent at understanding the buyer's source of financing. The good news was that his financier knew about the bankruptcy and was willing to move forward, so we closed the deal.

In reality, the first deal could have been closed had the buyer been forthcoming about the bankruptcy to the bank. The buyer just didn't think it mattered, but they were wrong. It wasn't that the bankruptcy was devastating to the first deal, but it was a surprise that undermined the sales process.

When it comes to due diligence, honesty and authenticity are *always* the best policy. The seller needs to fully acknowledge the depth of due diligence that a buyer needs to do, and both need to be supportive of each other. Due diligence is an ongoing research exercise to confirm the known and unknown. It is an exploratory process, and in many ways it's a partnership. For instance, the buyer might say, "There is a contract that we didn't know about. Now we need to go further into what the contract entails and who the parties involved are." As mentioned earlier, the goal is for the seller to tell the buyer about any major issues prior to entering into an LOI so that all the due diligence after LOI is confirmatory in nature.

Generally, there will be a deep dive into due diligence for the first three to four weeks after an LOI is signed. If a deal is going to fall apart, it will be during this time period, when something like a quality of earnings is being conducted. Or there might be new data being brought to the table that brings the transfer of ownership into question. After the quality of earnings is completed, due diligence will continue but will focus more on the peripherals instead of the core of the deal. For instance, due diligence might continue in the area of the supply chain.

TIME AND SURPRISE KILL DEALS

Deal fatigue is a real thing, so I'm sure you can understand that if a deal takes too long, it may never be consummated. In the same way that human beings can take only so much stress and churn, human beings also are resistant to change. To state the obvious, businesses are run by people who tend to look at the bottom line and care a lot about certainty. It should be no surprise then that not only time but also "surprise kills deals." However, there is a simple solution to avoiding surprises: disclosure goes both ways.

Most due diligence is done by the buyer on the seller. That's accepted. But as mentioned before, the seller rarely gets paid 100 percent cash on close. There might be an equity rollover, a seller financing, or an earnout. Moreover, most sellers really care about how the buyer will treat their employees after the deal is completed. So the quality of buyer is equally important. For instance, the seller will want to review such things as the type of benefit package provided for their employees. Is it aligned with the current market? Generous? Or not so good?

The due diligence process also includes how the buyer will fund the transaction. The seller may have no debt on the company, but the buyer might be planning to put a huge amount of debt on the company, which would be extremely important to understand if there was seller financing. If the seller is taking an equity rollover, they will want to know whether or not the buyer has been successful in their business. If not, why would the seller want to invest with the buyer going forward? The seller will want a solid understanding of who the buyer is and the likelihood of success, not only for the business transaction but also for the company going forward.

Once again there can be no surprises because surprises are not only annoying; they are also time-intensive. Time and surprises kill deals.

TYPES OF DUE DILIGENCE

FINANCIAL

First and foremost, you want to review all of your financial records for the last three to five years. When examining the company's finances *before* you go to market, you'll want to determine if the expenses include things that the buyer would not want to incur. As an M&A advisor, I'm often amazed what are termed "business expenses." I have seen everything from kids getting allowances to no-show employees being paid to several cars run through the company that really belong to family members of employees. The seller is going to review all of their own financial records in detail and reverse out anything that is not a true company expense. This is where EBITDA adjustments occur. The buyer is also looking for one-time income or expenses that are not likely to happen again. For example, your company has added $2 million to its bottom line in the current year. But that contract is now over and is unlikely to be renewed. That is something you want to disclose to the buyer so they realize the EBITDA is somewhat inflated.

The depth of a company's financial review is dependent upon the quality of the books and records that the seller keeps. The truth is that most privately held companies don't have audited financials. However, audited financials are something that make the buyer feel very comfortable because a third party has conducted an in-depth review of the company's financials.

However, even if the seller doesn't have audited financials, there is a process that has come to the forefront over the past ten years called a "quality of earnings." A quality of earnings is a process conducted by a third party, usually an accounting firm. The firm reviews the company's financial records to determine if there are any abnormalities, such as whether or not what is currently recorded could be expected to happen in the future.

COMMERCIAL

Commercial due diligence "is the process through which a buyer analyzes a target company from a commercial perspective. The aim of commercial due diligence is to provide the buyer with an overall context of the company, based on its positioning in its market(s), and how that is likely to evolve in the years ahead."[23] It can include such things as the company's mission and vision, management and employees, legal matters, all products and services, and marketing and competition information.

Both seller and buyer need to be fully informed of the company's exact products and services, how the company creates and distributes its products and services, and where and with whom the company does business. Here is a good analogy. Back in the 1800s, the horse and buggy was the main mode of transportation, and every driver had a buggy whip at their disposal. The company that made those buggy whips would have been a very valuable business, especially to a company that produced the buggies and was looking to grow its revenues through acquisition. However, in today's business climate, the buggy whip business would have a very limited market.

---

23   "What Is Commercial Due Diligence & How to Conduct It?," What is Commercial Due Diligence & How to Conduct It Properly, July 30, 2022, https://dealroom.net/faq/commercial-due-diligence.

I was recently involved in the sale of a company that installed ATMs. The company had been very successful; however, buyers were looking at it and saying, "Cash is going away. The company might still be a good business, but that doesn't seem to be the case for the long term." We had to show that the business was not just ATMs but also had a much broader scope and was capable of installing any kind of technology into walls, not just ATMs. This future story, which is part of commercial due diligence, ensures that buyers looking at a company don't walk away, saying, "This is a 'buggy whip' business." The last thing you want to hear is that *you* have a buggy whip company, so it's important that you can tell a credible future story.

OPERATIONS

A company's operations are another key area that sellers need to review so they can competently explain how their company works to potential buyers. This is examined in Phase 2 and more in depth in Phase 3. How does the company create/produce/deliver its products and services? Can and will the company continue day-to-day operations without the owner being present? Is there room for improvement that allows the buyer to make changes that will grow the company?

A company's information technology, or IT, is a good example of an operation that can make or break a sale. This is something that tends to be looked at in Phase 3. A company's IT includes any use of computers, electronic storage, networking hubs, and other physical devices and the infrastructure and processes to create, process, store, secure, and exchange any and all forms of electronic data, including telecommunications. Questions to be asked are the following: How up to date is the company's IT? Who is in charge of IT? Are there sufficient firewalls? Have there been any past breaches? If so, to what extent was the company exposed? Are employees allowed to take jump drives home containing company information to use on their personal computers? There is a plethora of other questions to ask, so both buyer and seller should have an IT expert on their team. Keep in mind that IT is one of the hot button topics that can kill a deal.

TAXES

We all know that Uncle Sam, federal and local, wants his hands in every financial cookie jar. When it comes to the sale of a company, both seller and buyer want to know the full extent of their tax exposure and how to limit that exposure. Having worked with companies throughout the nation, I can tell you there have been dramatic changes in local, state, and federal tax laws. This is another area where both seller and buyer should have an expert on their team. Even if you have a background in accounting or are a CPA, don't assume you know all there is to know when selling or buying a company.

HUMAN CAPITAL

In today's global business world, a company's human capital—how that company is staffed—has undergone tremendous changes. Salespeople conduct business via video conferencing. Business staff and employees often work remote full time or split their time between remote and in-office work. Questions to be asked are the following: How is the company staffed? What does the organization chart (org chart) look like? What does the reporting relationship look like? Are there open positions?

You might ask, "How does human capital affect the sale of a company?" Let's say that a business has an adjusted EBITDA of $4 million; however, a closer look at the org chart shows that 20 percent of job postings are unfilled. Are those jobs really necessary? If so, who is doing the work? What will the cost be to the buyer? Will the buyer need to revise the org chart? These are just some of the questions that need to be answered to account for all human capital.

RISK MANAGEMENT

Risk management is a fancy way of saying the word "insurance." Both seller and buyer need to know if the company has adequate insurance, including general liability, professional liability, errors and omissions, and whatever is applicable to that particular company. While I have never watched a deal die over risk management, both seller and buyer want to be clear on any legal liability issues.

LEGAL

Legal due diligence starts with what might seem to be a simple question: Does the seller have proper title to the company? Over the years I've sat with founders/owners who tell me they own their 100 percent of their company. But upon further review, there are individuals who were given a small percentage of the company in exchange for, or part of, doing particular work. These people haven't been heard of for years but suddenly show up when the company is for sale—and rightfully so—but these types of side deals can complicate the sale. The buyer wants to know if there are any ambiguities regarding ownership.

As well, the buyer wants to know if the company is legally qualified to do business in all the states in which it is operating.

Legal due diligence also includes understanding the regulations of the industry in which the company operates. For instance, if the company is a healthcare provider, HIPAA and Health Insurance Portability are extremely pertinent. But if the company is a construction firm, HIPAA isn't going to matter.

All business-related contracts are another area of legal concern. For example, some contracts are terminable upon there being a change of ownership. Perhaps the seller has twenty different contracts, each representing 5 percent of the company's revenue. However, if eighteen of those contracts are terminable upon a change of ownership, the financial risk is much greater to the buyer than might otherwise be understood.

LIFT OFF LESSONS

- Due diligence is critical whether you are selling or buying a business.
- Due diligence occurs in all three phases of selling a company.
- As the seller, your due diligence starts with making sure you have access to all the records for your company, and if you are missing any, then you do what is necessary to get the copies you need.
- The buyer wants to know your company's strengths and challenges, so there are no foolish questions in their mind.
- After the LOI is signed, extensive, confirmatory due diligence is performed, the key word being *confirmatory*.
- When it comes to due diligence, "honesty and authenticity" are *always* the best policy.

CHAPTER 11

HOW DO I TIME MY SALE?

When an owner/founder wanting to sell their company comes to me, inevitably, I'm asked the following two questions:

1. How long will the process take?
2. When should I bring my company to market?

I fully understand why these questions are asked. As the founder/owner, it has taken you time and thought to decide to sell your business. Maybe it was an agonizing process. But now that you've made the decision, you want the selling process to go smoothly and quickly so you can move on with your life. So let's look at these questions.

HOW LONG WILL THE PROCESS TAKE?

The answer to that question is ... it depends. I have worked on transactions that took as little as three and a half months and other deals that have taken as long as two full years.

Typically, a sale takes nine to twelve months. Overall, the length of the process depends on how long it takes to prepare a company for sale. I've had sellers hand me all necessary documents, and after a thorough review, we have taken their company to market within two weeks. This is fantastic but rare. I've had other sellers say, "You want a list of my contracts? I'll send you a photo of my whiteboard." Disorganized sellers will take longer to bring their company to market, as I've noted before.

The timing for Phase 2 has the most variation. Just like dating, a buyer and a seller may fall in love at first meeting and decide to move forward together. More common is for the seller to go out on a lot of dates over weeks and months. There can be a lot of "frog kissing" before the right buyer comes along.

We have seen this phase take anywhere from two months (rare) to two years (also rare). Typically, it takes three to six months to find a buyer and negotiate an LOI.

Once the LOI is signed, Phase 3 begins—the time period from LOI to closing. This usually takes 90 to 120 days. Sellers are often surprised that it takes months to get to a closing after the LOI is signed. As previously discussed, there is a lot of activity that happens in order to go from LOI to a closed transaction. This closing timeline is used to prepare sellers for the numerous workflows that occur in Phase 3.

To sum up, nine to twelve months for a sales process is normal, and three months longer or shorter is also common.

WHEN SHOULD I BRING MY COMPANY TO MARKET?

THE OWNER'S CONUNDRUM

When is the best time to sell your company? Usually when you least want to.

Let me explain.

Imagine a dark period for your business. You've lost some clients, and you do not see new ones in the short term. The trend in your industry is bleak. A former employee has filed a frivolous lawsuit, and a current employee is making unreasonable demands. You are exhausted and burned out and dream of doing something else.

This is not the time to sell. There will be few buyers and a reduced price. This is the time to buckle down and fix your company. In contrast, let's assume that your company is performing well. You have new clients, existing clients are renewing contracts, margins are improving, your employees are satisfied, and you are enjoying owning and running your company.

This is the time to sell, and this is the owner's conundrum: The very time you want to stay with your company is likely the best time to leave. And the very time you want to leave your company is actually the most important time to stay.

Remember, buyers want to step into your shoes, not into your problems.

IMPACT OF MACROECONOMIC FACTORS

Sellers often asked whether factors such as interest rates, inflation, recession, and changes in tax laws should impact their decision to bring their company to market. Sellers should be aware of what is going on in the larger world but base their decision mainly on the current and projected performance of their company. It is best to sell when you and your company are ready.

Some sellers hesitated to bring their companies to market in early 2022 because interest rates were increasing. However, we saw that rising interest rates had little to no impact on company valuations because there was a historic level of capital available for buyers.

Similarly, buyers were excited that there would be a flood of sellers seeking to transfer in 2021 because capital gains rates were projected to increase. (Rates did not increase.) In truth, buyers were not able to get "discounts" on selling companies because the number of interested buyers far exceeded the number of quality sellers.

Bottom line: be aware of what is happening in the world, but the most important considerations relate to you and your company.

RESIST THE URGE

It may seem strange, but there is a significant percentage of sellers who consider buying a company a year or two *prior* to bringing their company to market. Their thinking is, "My company is terrific, but it really needs one extra thing. So I'm going to buy another business that brings that one extra thing, which will improve the overall value of my company." If their company is worth $10 million today and another $2 million is spent to purchase another business, the goal is to sell their company for $14 million.

Reality and experience show this rarely happens. After an acquisition, the two companies need to be integrated. Employee benefits, payroll systems, accounting systems, invoicing for clients, and much more are all likely to be different, and it takes time to get all the pieces to work together. I caution sellers to *not* distract themselves by taking on an acquisition in the eighteen to twenty-four months prior to going to market.

To illustrate, my company was working with a seller for quite a while, and we were close to finalizing an LOI for over $50 million. A small competitor to the seller approached my client, seeking to be purchased. Amid negotiating the sale of my client, we opened a negotiation to purchase this competitor.

Not surprisingly, both negotiations—the sale and the purchase—took more time than my client expected. Further, when the acquisition closed, my client was caught between juggling the sale of their own company and the integration of the new company, and he became increasingly short-tempered and irritable.

Here's the sad part. The buyer of my client was pleased with the new acquisition but paid *no value for it*. In essence they said, "We like the purchase a lot, but we're not interested in changing the sale price we have offered for your company." My client spent their hard-earned money and had put in a huge amount of time and effort into a process that gave them no return.

LIFT OFF LESSONS

- While the sale of a company typically takes nine to twelve months, anywhere from three months to two years is possible.
- When is the best time to sell your company? Usually when you least want to.
- When deciding when to sell your company, be aware of what is happening in the world, but the most important considerations relate to you and your company.

CHAPTER 12

WHY SHOULD I HIRE AN M&A ADVISOR?

You've reached this chapter armed with a lot of information, hopefully a good education, and the knowledge you need to empower yourself. As Kofi Annan, former secretary-general of the United Nations, famously said, "Knowledge is power. Information is liberating. Education is the premise of progress, in every society, in every family."[24] Now you're asking the question, "Why should I hire an M&A advisor?" I'd like to answer that question by sharing this story.

I spoke with Howard, a business owner interested in selling his $30 million revenue company. While we got along well, after several discussions, Howard decided that he did not see sufficient value in having an M&A advisor. Since he had received advice and materials from me (and I imagine other M&A advisors) and had identified the

---

24   GPE Secretariat, "Kofi Annan Knew the Importance of Education," globalpartnership. org (Global Partnership for Education, August 24, 2018), https://www.globalpart-nership.org/blog/kofi-annan-knew-importance-education.

buyer, Howard was confident he could sell his company without an advisor. I wished him well but was concerned that it wouldn't go well.

Howard negotiated with his proposed buyer, and they entered an LOI. During due diligence, the buyer told Howard that he wanted to purchase the company in an asset purchase rather than a stock purchase. To make sure he was being "fair," the buyer was willing to pay an additional $50,000.

Howard called me after the closing and was ecstatic. Smart business owners, he claimed, could sell their companies without M&A advisors. Howard crowed that he found the buyer, he negotiated the LOI, and he actually *increased* the purchase price by $50,000 during due diligence.

I was impressed! But I was suspicious that costly errors had been made. The request for the asset purchase structure and the buyer's willingness to pay for this change raised alarm bells for me.

Usually, in an asset transaction, the seller tax bill is higher than it would be on a stock sale. Conversely, an asset transaction reduces the buyer's taxes. For reasons resulting from the complexity of the US tax code, the taxes the buyer will save over time are much higher than the seller will incur. In these situations the parties agree to the asset sale transaction, *but* the buyer pays the seller the amount of increased taxes. That way, the seller is held harmless, and the buyer gets a great benefit. A classic win-win.

At my request, Howard agreed that we could speak with his accountant. The three of us discussed the tax impact of asset or stock transaction issues. We quickly saw that Howard's taxes would increase by $140,000 in an asset sale and estimated that the buyer's taxes would be reduced by $2.5 million over time. Howard's $50,000 increased purchase price had cost him $140,000 in taxes.

During our discussion, I saw the closing balance sheet. It showed $3 million in cash being transferred from Howard to the buyer at close. When I asked why, Howard explained that cash was part of NWC, so it had to transfer. I replied that most sales are cash-free/debt-free transactions. The seller simply takes the cash on the balance sheet. Howard had lost $3 million.

It got even worse for Howard.

By including the cash on the balance sheet in the NWC calculation, the target NWC was greatly inflated. Even with the cash, it looked to me that Howard was going to have to pay the buyer in the NWC true-up in ninety days. Even more unfortunate, Howard was going to be responsible for the taxes on the revenue earned that led to the $3 million in the bank.

Without scratching the surface of the transaction, we found that Howard had lost over $4 million in value. But he did not pay a far smaller M&A advisory fee. The lesson from Howard's painful story is found in the saying, "Don't be penny wise and pound foolish."

ONE AND DONE

A depth of understanding gives you knowledge, and to quote Kofi Annan again, "Knowledge is power." Howard had neither understanding nor knowledge. He had one shot to make his sale a success. Howard learned that mistakes are expensive, and there are no "do-overs."

When you started your company, you likely had no idea how you were going to pull together all the elements of a successful business—finding customers, delivering goods or services, ensuring a profit, managing the operations such as accounting, HR, and the like. Every business owner looks back with amazement at what they did not know when they began and how much they learned along the way. Most are humble about the (many) mistakes made and what it took to fix them. This is why I begin every conversation with a successful business owner by offering my sincere congratulations. What you did was hard, and most people don't do it.

Selling your business is different—there is no learning curve.

Selling your precious business is a one-and-done proposition. Yes, you will learn a lot during the sales process, but unless you have a second company to sell, you're not going to have an opportunity to try to practice what you've learned. You don't want to be like Howard and lose a lot of money to avoid paying for support and experience.

TRUSTING AN EXPERIENCED M&A ADVISOR

Each transaction is unique. It's a unique combination of buyers, sellers, advisors, and business strengths and challenges. It's a kind of Rubik's Cube to be solved, and experience matters.

It's not easy to sell your company. It's not easy to run your company. And it is extremely hard to do both simultaneously. Your most important job is to keep your company running and growing.

You run your company and use the M&A advisor to lead the sale.

Don't let the process of selling your business distract you from your primary role. You lead your company and use the M&A advisor to lead the sale.

An experienced M&A advisor acts as a steady guide, taking you and your business through a journey that begins with your decision to sell. Your M&A advisor must be a trusted partner, and if you don't trust the M&A advisors that you interview, don't hire them. Find an advisor who has a great reputation, who has closed deals in your industry, who understands your personal goals, who "gets" what your business does, and who can give you a credible sense of how they will close a deal for you.

If you were getting a hip replacement, you would choose a doctor who has done hundreds of successful hip replacements, not just three. Why? Because you have one body, and you don't want to be experimented on. You want an expert, someone who's absolutely going to do the very best job possible.

Unfortunately, not all M&A advisors are proficient. It is crucial to check the qualifications of your M&A advisor to make sure this is someone you can have full confidence in. Any credible M&A advisor will have references from past clients who can tell you what it was like working with this advisor and that firm. Don't just hire your college roommate's brother in Ohio. You need an expert. You deserve an expert!

As you travel this road for what is most likely the only time in your life, you need someone who can lead the way. Yes, your feelings and preferences are important. But there will be times when your M&A advisor will have to "talk truth to power." They might cause you to readjust your price expectations because they know the market better than you do. They might push you to let the buyer meet a key employee or talk to a customer or two. They might recognize that you are letting your emotions get in the way of a more rational response that will advance your interests. You will need those kinds of guardrails and one-on-one talks.

IT'S EASIER TO KILL THAN TO CLOSE DEALS

There are an infinite number of pathways to failure and only a few to success. I've previously said *time kills deals*. In truth, it's not just time. Personality clashes can kill deals. Unrealistic demands and unsupported financial projections can kill deals. Problems exposed after signing an LOI that should have been disclosed pre-LOI can kill deals. Events that happen outside of your control—a government shutdown, a sudden heart attack of a buyer, a global pandemic—can kill deals.

Hiring an M&A advisor greatly increases the likelihood that the transaction will actually close. At sbLiftOff, we ensure that the transaction moves at an appropriate pace, smooth over personality differences, and prepare the parties about what to expect next. We have had transactions impacted by a government shutdown, health issues, and COVID-19, and we closed each one. I honestly don't believe any of these transactions would have closed without expert advice and execution.

IT'S NOT JUST MY OPINION

According to the National Center for the Middle Market, the leading academic resource focused on privately held companies with $10 million in revenue to over a billion in revenue:[25]

> Instead of taking advantage of the resources that exist to help, companies rely primarily on their internal teams and may be approaching buying and selling in an ad hoc fashion instead of in a strategic manner with the right advisors in place. As a result, many middle market companies discover that they are unprepared for the technical, financial, and integration-related aspects of the acquisition or sale, including keeping up with day-to-day management demands during the time when the transaction is underway.

25 "Middle Market M&A: What Executives and Advisors Need to Know to Make the Most of Mergers & Acquisitions," https://www.middlemarketcenter.org/ (National Center for the Middle Market, 2018), https://www.middlemarketcenter.org/Media/ Documents/best-practices-to-facilitate-more-successful-merger-and-acqusition-deals-in-the-future_NCMM_MA_Report_FINAL_web.pdf.

An article in the *Harvard Business Review* echoes these sentiments, noting,[26]

> About 10,000 middle-market companies are sold each year.... Middle-market leaders say that finding the right buyer for their company or the best target to acquire is one of the most confusing aspects of M&A. Nevertheless, they don't seek much help with the process. Both buyers and sellers of companies tend to rely heavily on their internal executives and top managers when searching for companies to buy or sell to. During the search process, about a third of buyers consulted an external law firm, and even fewer talked to consultants or investment bankers. Sellers were even less likely to bring in external advisors as part of their search for the right buyer.

The *Orlando Business Journal* states, "A common misconception is that M&A advisors simply exist to bring a buyer to the table. However, there are a myriad of pitfalls and unexpected costly hurdles during the selling process that could derail a successful exit without the counsel of an experienced advisor by your side."[27] *CEOWORLD* magazine affirms, "It takes an average of 1,000 hours to successfully

---

26 Richard Price, "Bridging the Gap Between Capital Providers and Midsize Companies," hbr.org (*Harvard Business Review*, May 3, 2021), https://hbr.org/2021/03/bridging-the-gap-between-capital-providers-and-midsize-companies.

27 Align BA, "10 Reasons to Hire an M&A Advisor before Undertaking a Middle-Market Business Transaction," bizjournals.com (*Orlando Business Journal*, March 4, 2022), https://www.bizjournals.com/orlando/partner-insights/navigating-ma-market-momentum/10-reasons-to-hire-an-m-a-advisor.html#:~:text=M%26A%20advisors%20will%20facilitate%20the,reason%20deals%20are%20re%2Dtraded.

close an M&A transaction." Then it asks the question, "Can you walk away from your business for 1,000 hours?"[28]

As a matter of interest, many ethical professional buyers seeking to purchase companies from sellers without M&A experience will insist, or strongly prefer, that the seller have an M&A advisor because it increases the likelihood of close.

M&A ADVISORS AND REALTORS: HOW THEY DIFFER

At this point you might be saying, "OK, I guess an M&A advisor is a little like getting a Realtor to sell my house," and you wouldn't be entirely wrong. There are some parallels. Realtors put a lot of time and some money for advertising, photography, marketing, etc. They only get paid if the house sells. If there is no sale, their time is lost, and expenditures are not reimbursed. Realtors know the risks involved, and the flat-rate compensation is their reward for taking that risk. Using a Realtor has become standard practice, and it is well understood that 86 percent of homeowners hire a Realtor when they sell their home, often a major family asset.[29]

But there are some signal differences between what a realtor does and what an M&A advisor does. First, as we've discussed, the deal must be kept confidential. This is not a situation where you put a For Sale sign out front of your business. When a buyer has been found, unlike in a common real estate transaction, none of the legal

---

28   Dena Jalbert, "Top 10 Reasons to Hire an M&A Advisor," ceoworld.biz
      (*CEOWORLD Magazine*, February 3, 2022), https://ceoworld.biz/2022/02/03/
      top-10-reasons-to-hire-an-ma-advisor/.

29   "Highlights from the Profile of Home Buyers and Sellers," www.
      nar.realtor (National Association of Realtors, October 31, 2016),
      https://www.nar.realtor/research-and-statistics/research-reports/
      highlights-from-the-profile-of-home-buyers-and-sellers.

documents are standard, and most will need to be negotiated in excruciating detail. For example, there are extensive structuring matters that can trigger tax, accounting, legal, and operating issues, all of which a proficient M&A advisor is well aware of.

M&A advisors are largely paid their fees upon success, and the majority of M&A advisory compensation is due only if the transaction closes. While it is true that advisors put countless hours into your transaction, the fee received if the deal doesn't close is minimal. Other professionals such as lawyers and accountants get paid whether or not a deal closes, while M&A advisors lose money on deals that don't close and therefore assume a great deal of risk.

I trust you can see that hiring an M&A advisor is best practice—for your business and yourself. Professional buyers and sellers in higher-priced markets would *never* consider any deal without competent M&A advisory; the risks are too great.

Hiring the right M&A advisor should pay for itself over the transaction timeline, increase the likelihood that your sale will close, and allow you to focus on running your company during the sale process. A competent and proficient M&A advisor should be a true partner in navigating all steps of the M&A process.

Bottom line: hiring an M&A advisor is worth the cost because you will save—or make—money in the long run.

LIFT OFF LESSONS

- As a successful business owner, you deserve sincere congratulations! What you did was hard, and most people don't do it.
- The M&A advisory fee is a small price to pay in order to avoid being penny wise and pound foolish.
- Don't let the process of selling your business distract you from your primary role. You lead your company and use the M&A advisor to lead the sale.

CHAPTER 13

HOW IS GOVCON DIFFERENT?

The advisors you work with need to understand and have experience in your industry. You wouldn't—or shouldn't—choose an accountant or lawyer outside your business sector. So make sure that you choose an M&A advisor who understands what you do and the world in which you live.

Providing goods and services to a government is different from providing those same goods and services to commercial, industrial, or residential markets. No client functions the same way government does. The process of obtaining work, getting paid, and responding to complex regulations is all different. Even if you work for just one government entity, such as the federal government, you will need to master complicated and intricate rules in order to be successful. If you work for state and local governments, you must master an even broader array of regulatory structures. This is not for the fainthearted.

My firm, sbLiftOff, works with federal government contractors (GovCon).[30] Most people don't know this, but much of the function of the federal government is actually performed by private sector companies, not government employees. GovCon companies are often quite mission driven. I've had clients who are completely focused on improving healthcare in the United States by building technology systems to allow doctors and hospital systems to communicate effectively. I had one client, a retired veteran, who wanted to continue his service to the country by managing multiple military bases. Other clients were committed to ensuring our national security by developing cutting-edge cybersecurity tools to protect the military and the State Department. SbLiftOff is honored to be able to serve these business owners.

The sbLiftOff team lives in the world of IDIQs, BIC contracts, BPAs, task awards, NAICS codes, five-year revenue averages, set-aside designations, and the like.[31] Our clients do not have to start by first describing how their world functions. We understand.

This chapter is written for GovCon companies to identify M&A considerations unique to their particular market. While I am mostly writing about federal GovCon companies, many of these observations are applicable to companies that provide goods and services to state and local governments.

---

30   For more information, go to https://www.sba.gov/business-guide/ grow-your-business/become-federal-contractor.

31   IDIQ—indefinite delivery/indefinite quantity; BIC—Best in Class; NAICS—North American Industry Classification Systems, https://www.census.gov/naics/ (accessed February 2, 2023).

GOVCON BUYERS

Buyers of GovCon companies should be deeply familiar with the GovCon sector. Selling your GovCon company to a buyer who lacks experience in this field is a challenging and usually an unsuccessful endeavor. It is hard enough for a buyer to learn all about your company to determine whether they want to move forward; doing that at the same time as learning about the GovCon world is nearly impossible.

STOCK VERSUS ASSET TRANSACTIONS

There are two ways to buy a company. The buyer can purchase all the assets of the selling entity and specify which liabilities, if any, are being transferred. The primary benefit of an asset purchase is the buyer avoids liabilities that might be tied to the company that are not expressly identified. An asset purchase transaction is the most common mode of transaction for companies with a purchase price of under $100 million.

The second transfer method is an equity sale. In this structure, the buyer purchases the stock or membership interests of the selling company. All assets and liabilities transfer with a stock transaction, and most buyers prefer to avoid stock purchases.

Virtually all GovCon transactions are done as stock purchases. For most of these companies, its value is in the contracts that have been won. If a GovCon company sells in an asset transfer, the government has to "novate" each contract. Novation means that the government needs to expressly agree to the transfer of the contract from the seller to the buyer. The novation process can take months or even years, and both the buyer and the seller want to avoid this process.

In a stock purchase, with rare exceptions, the government contracts transfer from the seller to the buyer as a matter of law. No specific approval from the government is required. For this reason most GovCon transactions are done as stock purchases, not asset transfers.

There is another benefit to stock transactions for GovCon companies. Important assets are its past performance (including CPARS) and ISO or CMMI certifications. Past performance and these certifications are critical when bidding on new contract opportunities. However, the government does not view past performance as an asset that can be individually transferred from one company to another. Similarly, certifications cannot be transferred as an asset. Both past performance and certifications transfer from the seller to the buyer in a stock transaction but not an asset acquisition.

SET-ASIDE DESIGNATIONS

The GovCon universe is divided into companies with set-aside designations[32] and those that compete in the "full and open" market. If your company has no designations, and all your work has been competitively bid and won,[33] your company will have a higher valuation than a company that has won its work with set-aside preferences.

The truth is, it's rare to find a GovCon company with under $30 million in revenue that does not have some set-aside designation

---

32 To help provide a level playing field for small businesses, the government limits competition for certain contracts to certain categories of businesses. Those contracts are called "small business set-asides," and they help small businesses compete for and win federal contracts. Source: https://www.sba.gov/federal-contracting/contracting-guide/types-contracts, accessed February 13, 2023.

33 An exception is that if your company wins sole-source contracts because you offer such a unique product or service, there truly are no other GovCon company competitors. This is rare but does happen.

with contracts won because of that designation. Getting started in GovCon is hard; as a matter of policy, the government provides some preferential treatment to certain groups.

SMALL BUSINESS

The broadest category are companies whose sole designation is "small business." These companies can be owned by anyone, so long as the company and its affiliates remain under specified revenue levels and/or employee numbers. The revenue and employee numbers are determined by the NAICS code applicable to your company's contracts. Companies with a small business designation are the easiest to transfer (outside the full and open world).

Avoiding "affiliation" between small business companies and other entities is probably the most significant issue in transferring these companies. Affiliation is a complex legal issue; do not attempt to figure it out yourself. Work with experienced counsel because inadvertently triggering an affiliation can cause a substantial decline in the value of your company. Ensuring that a transaction does not trigger affiliation issues has the effect of limiting the universe of buyers for companies with a small business designation.

VETERAN-OWNED COMPANIES

Veteran-owned companies—whether service-disabled veteran-owned small businesses (SDVOSB) or simply veteran-owned small businesses (VOSB)—must be owned and controlled by a US military veteran who meets the requirements. A veteran, or a group of veterans, must own at least 51 percent of the company.

Until recently, veterans could either be certified by the Veterans Administration as an SDVOSB or "self-certify." In 2021 Congress changed the rules and now requires express certification by the Small Business Administration. Companies previously approved by the Veterans Administration will continue to be recognized as authorized to operate as SDVOSBs. Because of this legal change, many self-certified SDVOSB companies will likely need to sell their companies in the next few years to veterans who can meet the rigorous requirements for government certification.

While less than 10 percent of the total US adult population are veterans,[34] they are well represented in government contracting. As a result, there is an active market for the purchase of veteran-owned businesses. Too many veterans have been told that they cannot transfer their business because of the SDVOSB or VOSB designation; this is just inaccurate and one more reason to work with advisors who deeply understand the set-aside GovCon market..

WOMEN-OWNED/MINORITY-OWNED COMPANIES

Women-owned and minority-owned businesses must be owned by people who meet the applicable designation. Unfortunately, there are fewer potential buyers with sufficient access to capital who satisfy the requirements for these categories. In some circumstances, these companies can be more challenging to transfer.

8(A) BUSINESS DEVELOPMENT PROGRAM

The 8(a) program is designed to help socially and economically disadvantaged small business owners gain access to set-aside contracts or sole-source award contracts. Unlike other set-aside designations, this program requires businesses to exit the program after nine years.

---

34   Katherine Schaeffer, "The Changing Face of America's Veteran Population," pewresearch.org (Pew Research Center, April 5, 2021), https://www.pewresearch.org/fact-tank/2021/04/05/the-changing-face-of-americas-veteran-population/.

At the end of that time, with limited exceptions, the graduated 8(a) is no longer eligible for these preferred contracts.

Because of the limited competition, 8(a) companies can generate revenue that might not be available to companies with other set-aside designations. However, because of the graduation requirement, many 8(a) companies are not able to continue operating after their contracts expire.

In contrast to the other designations, 8(a) companies are extremely difficult to sell. First, an 8(a) contract does not legally transfer in a stock purchase; contract novation is always required. Second, the nine-year life span for these companies makes them undesirable acquisitions; what buyer wants to pay for a company that will lose value on a specific date? Third, as complex as GovCon is generally, the rules for 8(a) are particularly onerous and confusing. We worked on one transaction of an 8(a) purchasing another 8(a) doing the same kind of work. We consulted with five different law firms to deal with regulatory questions and got five different answers. We then turned to the SBA for guidance, who essentially advised us that they did not know either.

The best buyer for an 8(a) company is usually a "Super 8(a)," a category available to certain Native American, Alaskan, or Hawaiian entities. These Super 8(a)s know they are often the only potential buyer, so their valuations tend to be very low.

SELLING A COMPANY WITH SET-ASIDE DESIGNATIONS

Because companies with set-aside designations can only maintain their designation if the buyer can step into the same category as the seller, the universe of potential buyers is smaller than for full and open companies. Often, entire categories of buyers are eliminated from consideration. A reduced buyer pool means that the value of companies with set-aside designations is lower.

GovCon companies with designations will generally get an EBITDA multiple of between 3 and 6. The same company in the full and open market can expect an EBITDA multiple of between 5 and 10 or more. There is real value to a GovCon business owner of obtaining full and open contracts: presenting buyers with more than 30 percent of revenue coming from full and open contracts begins to have a material impact on the value of your company.

Within thirty days of purchasing a company with set-aside designations, the buyer must report to the government on whether the company still meets the standard for the set-aside designation. This recertification requirement is the government's method for ensuring the ongoing integrity of the set-aside market.

If a set-aside company is acquired by a buyer that cannot satisfy the requirements for the designation, all is not lost. Generally, the buyer will be able to keep the contracts held by the seller at close and continue to generate revenue and profit from those contracts. However, the buyer is unlikely to be able to recompete those contracts. As a result, rather than valuing the selling company based upon a multiple of EBITDA, the buyer will pay the seller based upon the profits that are likely to be earned on the contracts in backlog at the time of closing. This valuation method—a variation of discounted cash flow—is likely to be materially lower than the valuation based upon an EBITDA multiple.

IMPACT OF SIZING OUT OF SET-ASIDE DESIGNATIONS

The general rule that larger companies with higher EBITDA get increased EBITDA multiples does not always apply in GovCon for companies with set-aside designations. As a set-aside company begins to approach its size out caps, the EBITDA multiple actually decreases.

For example, let's say there is a small business designation company working under a $30 million NAICS code. For purposes of this example, this company has a top-secret facilities clearance, has firm fixed-price contracts with terrific margins, and has exceptional CPAR. If the five-year revenue average is $12 million, this company will be valued using a 5 EBITDA multiple. With some structuring (seller financing, equity rollover, or earnout), the EBITDA multiple might even be higher. However, that same company with a five-year revenue average of $27 million is unlikely to get more than a 4 multiple.

"Why?" you might ask.

Making the move from set-aside contracts to full and open is risky. Many companies do successfully make this transition, but if the seller is looking to avoid this risk and pass it on to the buyer, there is a limited pool of buyers who are willing to take this on. And those buyers will price this risk into their valuation.

Please note that this means that the EBITDA multiple will be lower, not that the total valuation will be lower. For the company mentioned above, let's assume that the EBITDA for the $12 million revenue average is $2.4 million, while the EBITDA for the $27 million revenue average is $5.4 million. At a 6 multiple (which would be very high), the value for the smaller company will be approximately $14.4 million, and the value for the larger company will be approximately $21.6 million. So you still create more value by growing your company, but it is not proportionate. And you take the risk that you might not be able to fund a buyer willing to take on the risk.

This is an important point: many business owners manage their set-aside company to stay below their applicable size out five-year revenue average. It is the rare buyer—and I have yet to meet one—that is willing to purchase a company with the goal of maintaining its current size; virtually every buyer is seeking growth.

WHEN TO BRING A GOVCON COMPANY TO MARKET

A GovCon company is basically a portfolio of individual contracts and vehicles, and having a deep understanding of your backlog and the percentage of revenue coming from individual contracts is critical to determining when to go to market with your company.

If you have a recompete that represents a significant percentage of your revenue (and hence EBITDA) within the next twenty-four months, you will not get the same valuation that you would if you have just reloaded your backlog.

The time to bring your company to market is when you have maximized your contracted backlog and have at least a few months of experience involving any new contracts. This is a balancing act. On one hand, you want to be able to transfer the largest backlog you can. On the other hand, there needs to be at least a few months experience with new contracts, or recently won recompetes, to show actual margins on those contracts.

> **A GovCon company should have a backlog equal to at least two times the trailing twelve-month revenue of the company.**

As a very rough rule of thumb, a GovCon company should have a backlog equal to at least two times the trailing twelve-month revenue of the company. A company with a backlog equal to only the last twelve months of revenue should not go to market; buyer interest will be low. A company with three times the trailing twelve months of revenue will be highly sought after.

Project-based GovCon companies such as construction firms are an exception. Multiples for project-based companies are lower than for GovCon companies with long-term contracts. As a result, there is less focus on "backlog" and more on contract vehicles and depth of relationship with clients.

WHAT DRIVES VALUATIONS IN GOVCON

As discussed in chapter 6, companies get valued by calculating adjusted EBITDA (the science part of the valuation) and then determining the EBITDA multiple (the art part of the valuation). In GovCon, there are many factors that go into determining what the EBITDA multiple should be, such as the following:

1. Level of backlog
2. Sophistication of the goods or services provided
3. Facility clearances
4. ISO and CMMI certifications
5. Depth of relationship with customers (Are you responding to request for proposals, or are you working with the contracting officer to shape opportunities before they are generally released?)

Here is a chart that delineates just some of the factors that will impact the EBITDA multiple:

LOWER MULTIPLE (2x-4x)	HIGHER MULTIPLE (6x-8x)
Smaller Company Size (Low Enterprise Value)	**Larger** Company Size (High Enterprise Value)
Flat-to-Declining Financial Performance	**Growing** Financial Performance
Smaller Backlog (1-2 Years of Revenue)	**Larger** Backlog (3+ Years of Revenue)
Backlog is Primarily **Sub Work**	Backlog is Primarily **Prime Work**
Awarded Contracts are Primarily **Set-Asides**	Awarded Contracts are Primarily **Full & Open**
High Client/Contract Concentration	**Low** Client/Contract Concentration
Commodity-Type Services (e.g., IT Staffing)	**Mission-Critical** Capabilities & IP (e.g., Cybersecurity)
No Security Clearances Required	**Secret & Top Secret** Clearances Obtained
Limited Multiple Award Contracts (e.g., IDIQ, GWAC, BPA)	**Best in Class** Contract Vehicles (e.g., OASIS, ITES)
Outsourced BD & Proposal Team with **Low** Win Rates	**In-House** BD & Proposal Team with **High** Win Rates
HIGHER DISCOUNT RATE >30%	LOWER DISCOUNT RATE <15%

LIFT OFF LESSONS

- Work with M&A advisors who understand your industry.
- Virtually all GovCon transactions are done as stock purchases to avoid seeking government novation of contracts.
- The GovCon universe is divided into companies with set-aside designations and those that compete in the full and open market.
- Companies with set-aside designations are transferable at a lower EBITDA multiple than companies in the full and open market.
- 8(a) companies are particularly challenging to sell.
- Avoiding "affiliation" between small business companies and other entities is probably the most significant issue in transferring these companies. Affiliation is a complex legal issue; do not attempt to figure it out yourself.
- The general rule that larger companies with higher EBITDA get increased EBITDA multiples does not always apply in GovCon for companies with set-aside designations.

CONCLUSION

Congratulations! You now have a solid understanding of what it takes to sell your business and what the M&A process looks like. I hope you've enjoyed reading this book as much as I've enjoyed writing it.

I wrote it for you, answering the questions I've been asked time and again by business owners/founders like you. In this conclusion, please let me give you some parting advice.

First, I encourage you—I challenge you—to be the person you truly are. You have a viable business to sell. The market will determine the price range you can sell it at. Remain calm as you move through the M&A process. Figure out what would be a reasonable win—the price point—and particulars that are important to you, such as taking care of your employees. Determine what you truly need to feel satisfied with the outcome of the sale. If you get what you need, that's great! And if all of your wants are met, that's a bonus. But at the completion of the sale, don't say, "If I got that, then I should have asked for more." Just remember the Rolling Stones lyric, "You can't always get what you want. But if you try sometimes, you get what you need."

Make peace with the reality that fair market value exists. You can only sell your business for an amount that someone else is willing to give. Give a lot of thought to how you are going to position yourself psychologically and emotionally in the process. And please be thoughtful, kind, and empathetic to the other side. It's better for everyone. You'll get a more stable deal and a sense of satisfaction after the deal has closed.

Second, even if you're planning to sell your business years in the future, it's important to start benchmarking where you are today and target where you need to go. To do that, build your M&A team before you need them. Get advice and direction on your specific situation so when you are ready to go forward, you have already incorporated advice from your M&A advisor, lawyer, and accountant. Some of that team might be internal to your company. Determine if you can include your CFO in your planning. If not, determine how you will gather financial information that will be required. The more you can do to position your company for a successful transition to another owner, the better your sale price—and sale process—will be.

You are now armed with the high-level information you need to succeed. You understand the importance of regulating your emotions, expecting them and controlling your response to them. You know the importance of having the right team around you and the disadvantage of trying to do it all yourself.

With these assets, you are well ahead of other business owners in the market. Go forward and lift off successfully to your next goal in life!

Respectfully,
Sharon

ADDITIONAL RESOURCES

For more information, including models, charts, and graphics, follow the QR code below.

ACKNOWLEDGMENTS

I've received a great deal of support from many wonderful people to complete this book. I thank my collaborator, Simon Presland; my partner and best senior editor, Nancy Langer; and the entire team at sbLiftOff. I couldn't have done it without you!

I also want to thank my big sister, Helene Ballen; my son, David Heaton; and my mother, Ida Epstein, for their ongoing encouragement and inspiration.

Finally, I wouldn't be able to write a book like this if it hadn't been for all of our sbLiftOff clients—a tapestry of people across America—each of whom I've gotten close to and with whom I shared an emotional and life-changing journey.

ABOUT THE AUTHOR

Known as one of the country's leading small business advocates, Sharon Heaton, owner of sbLiftOff, is a frequent speaker and publishes in *Harvard Business Review, Forbes, Washington Business Journal,* and other outlets. She was named one of the 50 Most Influential Women in M&A by BDO and one of the Top 25 Women in M&A by Opus Connect.

"I founded sbLiftOff," says Heaton, "to serve those special people who sit at their kitchen table come up with an idea, start a business, hire people, pay their taxes, and fuel our economy. Small business owners are the backbone of the American economy, and we are honored to make sure they get a fair deal."

Before starting sbLiftOff, Heaton worked for the global law firms of Skadden Arps and Latham & Watkins, served as senior counsel on the Senate Committee on Banking, Housing, and Urban Affairs, and worked as general counsel and deputy staff director of the Senate Committee on Environment and Public Works. She cofounded Wellford Energy Group, an investment bank serving clean energy and low-carbon companies, and was also deputy counsel of a Fortune 500 company operating in ten states.

Heaton's company focuses on government contracting and commercial companies with $15 million to $100 million in revenue, known as the lower middle market, an underserved sector of the economy.

Sharon Heaton holds a juris doctorate from the University of Chicago Law School and a BA from Barnard College.